AN
ILLUSTRATED

LIFE OF JESUS

From the National Gallery of Art Collection

RICHARD I. ABRAMS
WARNER A. HUTCHINSON

ABINGDON
NASHVILLE

All reproductions of art in this book are from The National Gallery of Art in Washington, D.C. Each picture is fully described in an adjoining caption and listed in the index. Used with permission.

Design and Calligraphy: RICHARD A. OLSON

Art Consultant: TIMOTHY C. VERDON

An Illustrated Life of Jesus from the National Gallery of Art Collection. Copyright © 1982 by Richard I. Abrams and Warner A. Hutchinson.

First Edition

This book was set in Bembo typeface by Scarlett Letters, Inc.

Manufactured by Federated Lithographers-Printers, Inc. at Providence, Rhode Island, United States of America

Library of Congress Cataloging in Publication Data

Abrams, Richard I. (Richard Irwin), 1934–
    An illustrated life of Jesus.
    Includes index.
    1. Jesus Christ—Art. 2. Christian art and symbolism. 3. Jesus Christ—Biography. 4. Christian biography—Palestine. 5. National Gallery of Art (U.S.) I. Hutchinson, Warner A. (Warner Alton), 1929– II. National Gallery of Art (U.S.) III. Title.
N8050.A25   704.9′4853′0740153   81-17575   AACR2
ISBN 0-687-01356-9 Regular   ISBN 0-687-01358-5 Deluxe
ISBN 0-687-01357-7 Limited

INTRODUCTION

Over the centuries the story of Jesus has been told and retold in many ways. In the beginning, people who heard him teach or saw him work a miracle told their friends and relatives. Later the Four Evangelists—Matthew, Mark, Luke, and John—each wrote down his story of Jesus, drawn from the stories people told as well as what he himself remembered or selected from all that he saw and heard during the event-filled months he traveled with the Master. These four accounts, or Gospels, became the foundation for all the retelling of the story ever since.

At first most people did not have access to the written documents, and many did not know how to read even if the documents had been available. So the story of Jesus was told in sermons. Soon artists told it in paintings and sculpture. Musicians recounted it in song. Weavers used it as the theme for tapestry. Metalworkers took events from the story for their casting. Poets told it in meter. Glaziers fashioned brilliant windows to reflect the events and symbols found in the story. Translators made the story available in hundreds of languages. Wealthy patrons commissioned artists to use their genius to adorn churches, palaces, and homes with pictures of events from the life of Jesus.

An Illustrated Life of Jesus combines word and picture to enrich our appreciation of the continuing power of this story to stir both mind and heart. The National Gallery of Art collection includes one of the world's most impressive holdings of paintings and other art forms which depict events throughout the life of Jesus.

A number of the Gallery holdings shown in this book have not previously appeared in print. Others are so famous they are instantly recognizable. Although the illustrations are drawn from several centuries of art from medieval to contemporary times, the majority were created by Flemish, Renaissance, and Baroque masters. Representing the wide range of art media in the National Gallery of Art collection, this book includes examples of painting, sculpture, manuscript illumination, drawing, engraving and etching, metalwork, tapestry, and ceramics.

The narrative sections in the book retell in contemporary language the event in the life of Jesus which is illustrated by one or more artists. Each narrative gives the reader an orientation to the theme of the picture. The art panel about each picture gives information about the artist and leads the reader into seeing more clearly how the artist envisioned and retells the story in his unique way. Although each panel has been carefully researched to reflect artistic and historical accuracy, the primary aim of the art panel is to enable the reader to enrich his or her own understanding of the story of Jesus by meditating on the artist's insights into that wonder-filled story.

Special acknowledgment is given to J. Carter Brown, Ira Bartfield, Lynn Gould, and Theodore S. Amussen of The National Gallery of Art for their helpfulness, especially in opening holdings not at present displayed to the public and for making all reproductions available in a timely manner both for writing and for production.

CONTENTS

Birth and Childhood

The Annunciation

The young virgin Mary sat in her room, pondering the mystery of her womanhood, for she was betrothed to the carpenter and they were soon to be married. Suddenly a heavenly messenger, the angel Gabriel, appeared. Mary was startled.

The angel began his most unusual message with the words, "Hail, thou that art highly favored, the Lord is with thee!" This compliment stirred Mary's trembling heart even more.

Sensing Mary's fear, Gabriel spoke at once to calm her: "Fear not, Mary, for thou hast found favor with God." Mary listened with growing astonishment as Gabriel explained that God had chosen her to bear a son, who was to have the name Jesus (Yahweh saves). This son would be the very Son of God and would inherit the ancient throne of King David. He would rule without end over the nation of Israel, God's chosen people.

With each new revelation of her child's destiny Mary's astonishment grew, until she burst out: "How can this be, seeing I know not a man?" Gabriel's reply stretched Mary's faith to the limits. He told her that her son would be born by the power of God's Holy Spirit.

As the meaning of Gabriel's words unfolded, Mary was filled with awe that such an event could take place, and that she of all women should be the one chosen to give birth to the Son of God. Knowing the difficulties she would encounter in explaining her condition to Joseph and facing the likelihood of rejection by her family and community, Mary movingly and in complete faith submitted her will and her body to the purposes of the Lord: "Behold the handmaid of the Lord; be it unto me according to thy word."

THE ANNUNCIATION
Jan van Eyck (Flemish, 1380/1400-1441); Transferred from wood to canvas; 93.0 x 36.5 cm. (36.3 x 14.2 in.); Andrew W. Mellon Collection 1937

THE ANNUNCIATION—To the Gothic love of intricate detail and mystical symbolism, Jan van Eyck brought an eye for clear objectivity and a passion for highly detailed draftsmanship. In The Annunciation his love of intricacy, his attention to detail, and his use of gloriously rich colors can readily be seen in his treatment of Gabriel's wings and garments. Note the detail given even to the precious stones and pearls which line Gabriel's cape.

The painting is filled with symbols taken from the Hebrew scriptures and from the traditions of the church. The scenes in the inlaid marble pavement show David slaying Goliath, Samson pulling down the temple of Dagon, and all in a pattern which includes the twelve mystical signs of the zodiac, so beloved by medieval astrologers.

Mary's hands are held in the traditional pose of prayer as she accepts the will of God in trusting faith. The beauty of drapery of her full garment makes her a quiet equal to the heavenly messenger. The descent of the heavenly dove, representing the Holy Spirit, clearly positions Mary as the center of focus.

Van Eyck has aligned Mary directly behind a white lily (symbol of purity and of resurrection) and a book (quite possibly a book of prayers). In this way he uses the objects of daily life, together with such architectural forms as arches and pillars, to express a mystical and invisible world of revelation and faith.

THE ANNUNCIATION
Fra Filippo Lippi (Florentine c. 1406-1469); Painting on wood; 103.0 x 163.0 cm. (40.2 x 63.6 in.);
Samuel H. Kress Collection 1943

THE ANNUNCIATION—A Carmelite monk, Fra Filippo Lippi was an influential Florentine painter in the fifteenth century. Toward the middle of the century he and Fra Angelico collaborated on a number of important works for the church in Florence and for the Medici and other noble families. So respected for his art was Fra Filippo that Pope Pius II released him and a nun, named Lucrezia Buti, from their vows so they could get married.

In The Annunciation the artist blends the hard and dark forms and spaces of the building with the luminous and fluid figures of the angel and the Virgin. Gabriel's wings are made from the feathers of a peacock, a royal and exotic bird of great value. He holds a stylized lily, symbol of purity and resurrection. Above Gabriel's head hovers a graceful dove, representing the Holy Spirit, whose rays shine directly on Mary.

Mary's eyes are downcast as she listens to the stranger's words, wondering what to make of them. The angel, respectful and courteous with partly bowed head, looks up at her, awaiting her response to his astounding message. Fra Filippo sublimely captures this moment of message and faith, and, from his perspective, the future of the world depends on what happens next in this quiet and remote setting.

Mary Visits Elizabeth

Mary's aged cousin, Elizabeth, was married to a priest named Zacharias and lived in the hill country of Judea. Their marriage was childless, and Elizabeth was now well beyond child-bearing years.

One day while Zacharias performed his priestly duties alone in the Holy Place within the Temple in Jerusalem, the angel Gabriel appeared to him, announcing that Elizabeth would soon conceive a child. This child was to be named John, and would become the forerunner of the Messiah. In stunned disbelief Zacharias expressed his doubt that such an event could ever happen. He reminded the angel that he and his wife were well past the age for having children.

Gabriel reprimanded Zacharias for his lack of faith, telling him that from that moment on he would be unable to speak until he named the child John. Furthermore, the God who was able to open Sarah's womb when she was past ninety, and so give Abraham a son who would be one of the fathers of the Israelite people, could readily enable Elizabeth to conceive a son who would announce the coming of God's Anointed One to his people. Speechless, Zacharias left the Temple, able only to make signs to the waiting worshippers, and returned to his home in Judea.

When Elizabeth was about six months pregnant, her young cousin Mary visited her. As Mary called out her greeting, the baby leaped in Elizabeth's womb. The Holy Spirit filled Elizabeth with joy and insight at that moment, enabling her to perceive the momentous event that had just occurred. This was not just two unknown and unimportant country women, both carrying babies, meeting in a remote corner of the world. Here was the future mother of the Messiah's forerunner meeting the future mother of the Messiah himself. In a flash of revelation and exultation Elizabeth cried out to Mary, "Blessed art thou among women, and blessed is the fruit of thy womb."

Rejoicing in her cousin's love and faith, Mary expressed the fullness of her heart in a moving poem of submission to the will of God and hope in the future. Mary stayed on with Elizabeth for three months and then returned to her home in Nazareth. How she and Elizabeth must have talked, during those quiet months together, about the lives their sons would lead!

THE VISITATION—Master E.S. was an engraver who worked in the vicinity of Lake Constance during the middle of the fifteenth century. He is known only by his initials which appear in some of his engravings. Master E.S. most probably was trained as a goldsmith, for his work shows the decorative nature and characteristic line of a goldsmith of that time. The mood of his work is Gothic, and he uses a graceful, nervous line to engage the viewer's feelings.

In The Visitation, Master E.S. shows the meeting between Mary and her aged cousin Elizabeth. Both women are clearly pregnant. Their wimples or headcloths visually echo the women's halos. Mary is demure

THE VISITATION
Master E.S. (German active c. 1450-1467); Engraving; 9.1 x 6.4 cm. (3.5 x 2.5 in.); Rosenwald Collection

and modest. Her left hand reaching out to grasp Elizabeth shows the depth of her personal need for understanding and support at this moment. Elizabeth reassures her as she holds Mary's right hand in both of hers. Elizabeth's face is filled with concern and caring as she welcomes the younger woman. This is a tender beginning to a welcome visit.

Gothic art is filled with animals, often suggestive of popular collections of fables about animals and birds which conclude with a moral. Master E.S. shows a bird above a rock behind the Virgin. Is this a symbol of the Holy Spirit? In the mid-ground a hare sprints off to the side.

BIRTH OF JOHN THE BAPTIST
Nicolo da Bologna (Bolognese, Late XIV Century); Illumination, initial 'n' from a choir book;
25.8 x 22.5 cm. (10.1 x 8.8 in.); Rosenwald Collection

BIRTH OF JOHN THE BAP-TIST—Nicolo was an illuminator in a scriptorium in Bologna during the second half of the fourteenth century. An illumination is a colorful, hand-painted embellishment of an initial letter in medieval manuscripts. Biblical or allegorical themes were often portrayed in these delicate miniature paintings. Because of the skills of Nicolo and a few of his contemporaries, Bologna became a center for Italian manuscript illumination for 150 years.

One of the notable elements of Bolognese illumination was the use of foliage as a decorative border for the tiny painting. In the Birth of John the illuminator shows the aged Elizabeth dressed in white with a golden halo. She sits in bed, leaning against a large bolster. Two maidservants tend the child, who lies in a cradle on the floor. He too has a golden halo. A young neighbor or family member stands by the bedside. Elizabeth is in some discomfort, her brow furrowed as she holds her head and grimaces. Her young friend is anxious and concerned. The maidservants show tenderness and sweet affection as they care for John. It is astonishing how many emotions the artist could convey in such a small space tucked inside the letter 'n' on a manuscript.

Ever since Zacharias' speechless return from Jerusalem, his writing out the account of the angel's message, and then Elizabeth's unexpected conception, the whole community had awaited the birth of the child with great eagerness. Neighbors and relatives rejoiced with the aged couple over the safe delivery of their son.

On the eighth day, according to Jewish custom, the boy was circumcised and named. Since he was the son of a priest who was himself of priestly lineage, it was assumed by all that the child too would become a priest. The priesthood was a privileged calling, affording community respect, material comfort, and the personal satisfactions which come from serving both God and man. Naturally it was assumed that the boy would bear a priestly name honoring his family tradition as well as his future calling.

At his circumcision the elders were about to name the boy Zacharias after his father and the venerated prophet, when Elizabeth intervened and insisted that the child be named John. It was not normally a woman's place to instruct the elders, but the boy's father could not speak. The elders reminded her that no one in the family had ever been named John, but she was adamant. As they turned to Zacharias for his opinion, he took out a writing tablet and wrote in large letters for all to see: "His name is John."

Astonished at this break in family tradition, the elders reluctantly gave in to the wishes of the aged couple. As soon as the elders pronounced the boy's name to be John, Zacharias' tongue was freed, and he praised God and rejoiced greatly with his friends.

Mary and Joseph

With embarrassment and difficulty, Mary told Joseph about the angel's visit and the impending birth of a child. Joseph could not understand how Mary could be with child while remaining a virgin, and yet he knew he loved her deeply. In his opinion marriage no longer seemed a possibility because of the nature of the society in which they lived. Still, he wanted to protect her as much as he could from any scandal.

According to the custom of that time, betrothal was the first legal step of marriage. A man and woman would not usually live together during their engagement, although their families had made binding commitments to one another. After an engagement period of about one year, a marriage ceremony sealed the betrothal commitments, and the couple began living together.

A divorce proceeding was required to break an engagement as well as dissolve a marriage. In a state of anguish Joseph reluctantly decided to divorce Mary privately to protect her reputation. However, before he could carry out his decision, an angel appeared to him in a dream and said, "Joseph, thou son of David, fear not to take unto thee Mary thy wife: for that which is conceived in her is of the Holy Ghost. And she shall bring forth a son, and thou shalt call his name JESUS: for he shall save his people from their sins." The angel further made it clear to Joseph that this wondrous event was in fulfillment of prophecies given long before.

When Joseph awoke, he considered carefully what the angel had said. It confirmed everything Mary had told him. Without delay, Joseph made arrangements for his marriage to Mary to be solemnized. They celebrated not only their love for each other but also the grandeur of what God was about to do through them.

THE MARRIAGE OF THE VIRGIN
Bernaert van Orley (Flemish, c. 1488-1541); Painting on wood; 53.7 x 32.3 cm.
(20.9 x 12.6 in.); Samuel H. Kress Collection 1952

Are Married

THE MARRIAGE OF THE VIR-GIN—Bernaert van Orley was considered the "official" painter of Antwerp during the height of his powers in the early sixteenth century. Although he did not specialize in portraits, he had great skill in creating psychological studies of personalities in his paintings.

In The Marriage of the Virgin, van Orley shows Mary and Joseph each lost in introspection about the significance of their situation. Mary is pregnant by the Holy Spirit, destined to give birth to the Messiah according to the word of an archangel. Little wonder she is in profound reverie. Her left hand symbolically rests on her womb where the infant Jesus is being formed. Joseph believes what the angel has told him of Mary's condition, but he also knows how women in small towns count the months between a marriage and the birth of the first child. He has Mary's reputation to protect. He knows also the heavy responsibility he will bear as the foster father of God's Anointed One. This marriage is no easy step for Joseph, regardless of the depth of his love for Mary. The weight and the solemnity of the occasion are obvious on both their faces.

The priest has performed his ritual obligation in a professional manner. The wedding guests are separated by sex, typical of ancient Jewish custom and of contemporary Flemish social occasions. Since the guests are talking, the ceremony appears to have just ended with the priest wishing the couple well in their new life together. Is there a touch of gossip among the wedding guests being suggested by the artist?

Van Orley's Gothic origins are revealed in the gargoyles which flank the bridal couple, while his Italian tendencies are reflected in the classical facade behind the couple. The arch above them and their joined hands bind Mary and Joseph together, even though the thoughts of each are intensely private.

The Birth of Jesus

THE NATIVITY
Fra Filippo Lippi and Assistant (Florentine, c. 1406-1469); Painting on wood; 24.0 x 58.0 cm.
(9.4 x 22.6 in.); Samuel H. Kress Collection 1939

In far-off Rome, alien center of imperial power, Caesar Augustus ordered a census to be taken in his unruly province of Palestine. The Romans were orderly administrators who wanted to know the human and financial resources of each of their provinces in order to best serve the overall interests of their empire. Once given, the order had to slowly work its way through the bureaucratic channels of Imperial Rome until at last it touched the lives of Mary and Joseph in the tiny hill village of Nazareth in Galilee.

Mary and Joseph were required to travel about one hundred miles south to the even tinier village of Bethlehem in Judea to register for the census. The census was to be a reckoning by households; and since Joseph was a descendant of King David, he and his family had to travel to David's ancestral home for the enrolling.

Even though Mary was close to delivering her child, she was determined to accompany her husband. Each day of the arduous trip Joseph made arrangements for an untimely delivery, hoping all the while that labor would not start until they were settled in a room in Bethlehem.

When at last they arrived, the town was crowded with families who had come from all over the country for the enrollment. At first Joseph was irritated that he could not readily find a room; but then, as he went from place to place without success, his irritation turned to a growing anxiety. Finally, in desperation he located an empty cave in a hillside just outside the town which was used to stable domestic animals. By this time Mary's labor had begun.

Joseph settled his young wife in a dry corner, trying to make her as comfortable as possible. Alone together, they delivered their firstborn child. Mary may have assisted other women in the past, but now she had only her own innate knowledge and Joseph's loving help. Soon the child was safely wrapped in clean binding cloths and laid gently in a manger. He fell asleep after having his first meal. For the first time since hearing that they would have to go to Bethlehem, Mary and Joseph relaxed. Jesus, Son of David and Son of God, was born.

THE ADORATION OF THE CHILD—Domenico Gagini was an Italian sculptor and architect during the second half of the fifteenth century. Although he worked at times in Florence and Rome, he was best known for his activity in northern Italy.

In his marble relief of the Nativity, Gagini demonstrates a gentle and delicate hand with his Madonna and the adoring angels. High above the Holy Family, God the Father rules in highest heaven. He holds the orb, symbolizing the created world, in his left hand and raises his right hand in blessing the infant Jesus. God is surrounded by legions of angels trumpeting the good news of Jesus' birth. The Holy Spirit is depicted as a dove hovering between heaven and earth, whose rays descend onto the Holy Family. Beneath the dove a chorus of angels sing "Gloria in Excelsis Deo." To the left an ox listens attentively while an ass munches fodder.

A stream, possibly representing the River of Life from the Book of the Revelation of St. John, flows down from the scene of the Nativity. A pair of joyful fish leap high in the air as they, too, celebrate the birth of the child. Three angels stand in worship on either side of the panel. They seem to float in the air even though their feet rest on the ground. One can sense they would leave no footprints.

*THE ADORATION
OF THE CHILD*
Domenico Gagini (Lombard, c. 1448-1492); White marble relief; 90.2 x 52.0 cm. (35.2 x 20.3 in.); Samuel H. Kress Collection 1937

THE ADORATION OF THE CHILD
Andrea della Robbia (Florentine, 1435-1525); Sculpture: glazed terra-cotta relief; 127.8 x 77.4 cm. (49.8 x 30.2 in.); Samuel H. Kress Collection 1960

THE ADORATION OF THE CHILD—The della Robbia family of Florence created some of the most exquisite enameled terra-cotta ceramics ever made. Luca della Robbia was the master who first perfected a technique for putting lead glazes to terra-cotta. This secret process he taught members of his family, including his nephew Andrea.

Andrea della Robbia was a prolific worker and a very popular artist in a city whose rich patrons appreciated his skills. His work ranged from superficial ornamentation to objects of great beauty, skill, and sensitivity.

In this glazed terra-cotta relief Andrea portrays Mary in a posture of worship before the infant Jesus. The white lilies are traditional symbols of her purity and his resurrection from the dead. The mother and child are guarded by two cherubs, reminiscent of the scripture which says, "He shall give his angels charge over thee." Yet these angels are more charming than fearsome, and perhaps were modeled after living children.

The hands holding a crown suggest Mary's future role as Queen of Heaven, a traditional theme of Marian piety. Mary's face has the fine lines of a Florentine patrician. She is very much a woman of this world, albeit devout; a woman whose presence would not disturb the comfort and social position of the leading families of Florence. The heraldic crest at the bottom of the ceramic indicates the patron for whom the relief was done; its cross and mitre probably denote a noble prelate.

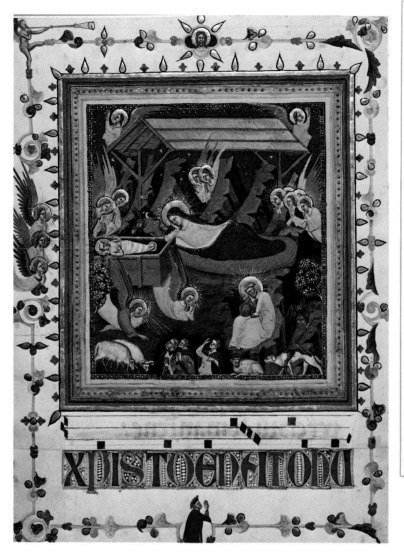

NATIVITY—This early fourteenth century work by an anonymous Florentine illuminator reflects the influence of Byzantine icons through its composition and treatment of individual figures. We see the same influence, tempered, however, by a new vision in Giotto's Madonna and Child on page 37. Compare the two works of art.

In this nativity scene Mary rests after giving birth, and there is wonder in her mind and heart as she gazes at Jesus. Joseph also rests at the foot of the manger. Shown smaller than Mary, he is less important in the hagiology of the church. This is her special moment, and she is central to the composition of the scene.

Angels, representing the entire host of heaven, surround the Holy Family and are even placed outside the frame. Some of them announce the birth of Jesus to the shepherds in the fields. While the sheep graze and a mountain goat or ram reaches for a succulent branch, a faithful sheep dog bristles at a menacing predator.

The illuminator places the glorified Jesus in a quatrefoil above the frame. To his right an angelic trumpeter sounds his horn. At the bottom of the frame a praying donor—a member of the church still in this world—is also at worship during this moment of nativity.

NATIVITY
Master of the Dominican Effigies (Florentine, c. 1340); Illumination leaf from a choir book; 36.4 x 27.1 cm. (14.2 x 10.6 in.); Rosenwald Collection

THE NATIVITY—An apprentice of the great Jan van Eyck, Petrus Christus was an active member of the Flemish school in Northern Europe. He often signed his paintings "XPI," the Greek abbreviation of "Christus" or "Christ."

In his The Nativity, Christus shows the Holy family in a large, rather static space. Joseph has taken his wooden clogs off in the presence of the divine child. He has doffed his hat and leans heavily on his staff. His young wife adores the infant, who emits rays of glory. Angels, more feminine than masculine, surround the child, their hands in the medieval attitude of prayer.

The town of Bethlehem is seen on the distant hills, and a flock of sheep are herded along a road. Some of the shepherds have left the herd to look in at the family. One of them glances at the child, as the others talk among themselves of what they have seen and heard.

Christus places this scene in an arch with late Gothic statuary. Adam and Eve stand on pedestals, and above them are depicted events from the opening chapters of Genesis, which tell how mankind's first parents disobeyed the will of God. According to Christian tradition, their Fall led to their expulsion from Eden and to the whole unhappy sequence of human sinfulness. God in his goodness, however, promised to send one who would someday come to redeem. Christus links this story with the birth of Jesus as that promised redeemer.

THE NATIVITY
Petrus Christus (Flemish, c. 1410-1472/73); Painting on wood; 130.0 x 97.0 cm. (50.7 x 37.8 in.); Andrew W. Mellon Collection 1961

The Shepherds' Visit

For centuries the wealth of Israel lay in its herds of sheep. The men who guarded the flocks from predators and who guided them to pasture and water were honored by all as men of integrity, courage, and compassion. They knew their sheep, often by name; they loved their sheep, often risking their own lives to keep them safe. So highly esteemed was the work of the shepherd that the prophets and psalmists often spoke of God as the Great Shepherd of his people.

By the time of the birth of Jesus, the traditions of a nomadic people tending its herds of sheep had been largely replaced by the alien urban cultures of Greece and Rome. Shepherds were now seen as lowly keepers of animals and relegated to the fringes of influence.

Yet it was to a group of shepherds in a field near Bethlehem that God first chose to announce the advent of the great Shepherd-King, the Messiah. It was a clear, cool night, and the shepherds were watching quietly over their flocks. Suddenly the sky was ablaze with light. An angel appeared before them. Calming their fears, the angel told the shepherds that the Messiah had just been born and was at that moment lying nearby in a manger in Bethlehem.

Then, tier upon tier of angels appeared in the sky. The shepherds heard them singing: "Glory to God in the highest, and on earth peace, good will toward men." Just as suddenly, the heavenly company vanished, leaving only the memory of the sight and the echo of the sounds.

Having regained their composure, the shepherds decided to seek out the child and pay him homage. Finally they found Mary and Joseph with the baby lying in a manger, just as the angel had said. They told the child's parents about the angel's visit and the appearance of the heavenly host. It was a moment that Mary and Joseph would never forget; and how it must have struck a responsive chord years later when Mary heard Jesus refer to himself as the Good Shepherd.

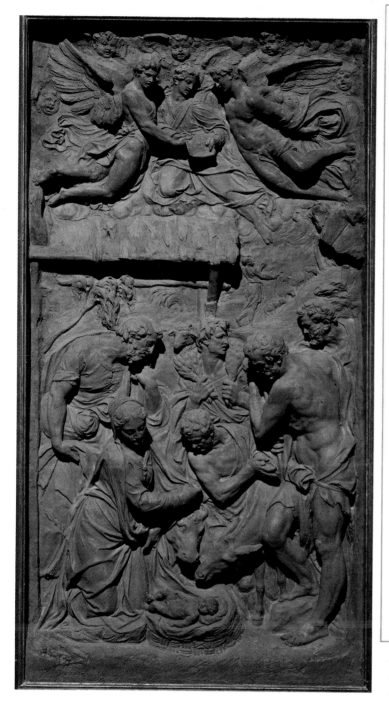

ADORATION OF THE SHEPHERDS

ADORATION OF THE SHEPHERDS —A Milanese sculptor, gem carver, and medalist, Annibale Fontana was noted for his skill in fashioning intricate scenes on precious stones and metals. He created vases, coffers, bowls, and medals which were much in demand, and often portrayed biblical events. A child of the Catholic Counter Reformation, he typically infused his art with moralistic themes.

The Adoration of the Shepherds is a terra-cotta ceramic which draws heavily on the classical Greek and Roman models which were so popular at the time of the High Renaissance.

The shepherds are drawn more from the tradition of naked Greek athletes than from any realistic notion of what shepherds look like. Even their tattered draperies are carefully molded to reveal the beauty of their physiques. The shepherds have rushed from the nearby field, seen on the hill in the distance, to see the child. Fontana shows them having to compete with the stable animals who crowd in for their own look at the child. A younger-than-usual Joseph stands behind Mary, peering over her shoulder. Mary's pose creates some space for the child, but she too is caught up in the shepherds' intense adoration.

Above the worshipers the angels hover and sing their paean of praise to the child. What angels actually look like is not known. They sometimes are reported appearing in the guise of a man. Because they could appear in the air, they were shown in some traditions of Western painting as creatures with wings. Here Fontana gives the major angels luxuriant wings and fully molded male bodies, while he gives the minor angels tiny wings and only the faces of adorable children.

The child, though the focus of every glance, is not the focus of the scene. Fontana looks more at those who worship the child than at the child who is being worshiped.

ADORATION OF THE SHEPHERDS
Annibale Fontana (Lombard 1540-1587); Terra-cotta sculpture relief; 109.0 x 57.0 cm. (42.5 x 22.2 in.); Samuel H. Kress Collection 1939

THE ADORATION OF THE SHEPHERDS— Giorgio da Castelfranco, generally called Giorgione, was a Venetian painter who died in his early thirties during the time of the Black Death in Venice. He was loved by his contemporaries as much for his lute playing and sweet singing at social gatherings as he was for his splendid paintings. Giorgione was greatly influenced by the great Leonardo da Vinci, and brought to his art a sense of lyric mystery.

In The Adoration of the Shepherds, the artist places the Holy Family at the entrance of a cave in a steep hillside. Deep inside the cave two cows eat from a pile of hay, while above the entrance tiny angels, almost invisible, protect the family from harm. The two shepherds have come to bow in worship before the child. Mary has taken Jesus from the manger and laid him in the sun. She folds her hands in prayer and wonder as she hears the story the shepherds tell of seeing angelic hosts singing in the night skies.

The shepherds are dressed in rags, tattered and stitched together in pieces. Just down the hill some of their companions watch over the flock as the sheep graze near a running brook. The central focus of the painting is the infant Jesus, who alone is not in shadow. It is as though the world paused for this one moment of adoration before going on its routine ways.

THE ADORATION OF THE SHEPHERDS
Giorgione (Venetian, c. 1478-1510); Painting on wood; 91.0 x 111.0 cm. (35.5 x 43.3 in.); Samuel H. Kress Collection 1952

The Presentation

When their infant son was forty days old, Joseph and Mary carried him six joyous miles to the Temple in Jerusalem. Once there, they prepared to perform two religious duties imposed on all Jewish parents from the earliest days of the Israelite people.

When a woman gave birth to a male child, she was considered ceremonially unclean for a period of seven days, and was forbidden to enter the sanctuary of the Temple for an additional thirty-three days. On the fortieth day the woman was required to offer a young lamb as a burnt offering and a pigeon as a sin offering. If, however, the woman had little means, she could substitute a second pigeon for the lamb.

Joseph's financial resources had been largely exhausted by the trip to Bethlehem, as well as by the necessity of paying rent once there, so that he could not afford a lamb for Mary's purification offering. Therefore he purchased two pigeons in the Temple courtyard and took them to the priests for sacrifice on Mary's behalf.

When the firstborn was a male, Jewish tradition required that the child be dedicated to the service of God, as though the child belonged to God himself. Those firstborn of the tribe of Levi had to devote their lives to religious service, while those born into other tribes had to be redeemed from such service by the payment of five shekels. Joseph had carefully saved five shekels for this most important occasion.

As the family entered the Temple grounds, they were met by an old man named Simeon. Many years before, God had come to Simeon and promised that he would live to see the Messiah with his own eyes. That morning, prompted by the Holy Spirit, Simeon came to the Temple. As he held the infant Jesus, he knew that at long last God's promise had been fulfilled. Simeon spoke to the Holy Couple of the blessing the child would bring to countless numbers, of the suffering he would undergo, of the hostility he would encounter, and of the anguish that Mary would one day experience.

An aged and pious widow named Anna soon joined Simeon and the Holy Family. She too announced to anyone who would listen that God's great day of deliverance had come at long last.

With the words of Anna and Simeon ringing in their ears, Mary and Joseph made their offerings, Mary presenting two pigeons and expressing her thanks to God for a safe delivery and the wonderful blessing manifest through her, while Joseph paid the five shekels and gave thanks to the Lord for the opportunity of raising as his own son the long-promised Messiah.

THE PRESENTATION IN THE TEMPLE

Hans Memling (Flemish, c. 1430/35-1494); Painting on wood; 59.8 x 48.3 cm. (23.3 x 18.8 in.); Samuel H. Kress Collection 1961

THE PRESENTATION IN THE TEMPLE—Although German-born, Hans Memling spent his professional life in the Flemish art center of Bruges. He traveled extensively, painting and studying in Spain, England, and Italy. He was an extremely popular as well as prolific artist.

In The Presentation in the Temple, Memling shows both his love of color and his attention to architectural detail. In this work Mary and the aged Joseph bring the newborn Jesus to the priest in the Temple to be named, circumcised, and blessed. Memling in his major works characteristically depicted Mary as formal, even austere. Here he shows her not as an affectionate young mother, but as she would appear at the foot of the cross, which Simeon alludes to in his prophecy. Her face is controlled, thoughtful, spiritual, and silent. She more than the child is the focus of this moment. Only she bears the halo.

The group watches her pass the child to the priest. The two young women are aristocratic, but charming rather than imposing. Dressed in fine clothes, wearing brilliant jewels, bearing themselves with self-assured stylishness, they are the pleasantly attractive people whom Memling often painted. The women are doubtless patron portraits, for Memling often included his patrons in his art. Each silent participant in the scene projects a sense of reserve; in this way Memling suggests the individual worth and uniqueness of each one who stands before the Christ Child and the Virgin Mother.

The Visit of the Magi

Far away in Persia there lived a priestly caste of scholars called Magi. The Magi steeped themselves in the lore of astrology to better understand the connections between the movements of the stars and historical events. It was just at this time that they interpreted the confluence of the stars and planets to signify that a great new king was about to be born in Judea. Convinced of the historic importance of this new king, the Magi set out to pay him homage.

Tradition tells us that there were three Magi who set forth on the journey, probably because of the three gifts of myrrh, frankincense, and gold mentioned by Matthew. Tradition has also invented the names of Melchior, Caspar, and Balthasar. We do not know whether they traveled by camel or horse, or from what city they came. However, they did appear unexpectedly at the court of King Herod, inquiring about the birth of a great new king.

Herod, villainous and bloody, feared for the safety of his own throne. He was not a Jew and was uncertain of the loyalties of his people. The Jewish religious leaders told him that the Scriptures placed the birth of the Messiah in Bethlehem. Herod urged the Magi to go to Bethlehem and, if they found the infant king, to report back to him so that he too could come and pay homage. In fact, Herod's real intention was to destroy the child.

As the Magi traveled south to Bethlehem, where the Holy Family was now living, they were guided miraculously by a star to the very house where Mary cared for Jesus. Paying their obeisance to the child, they lavished their rich gifts upon the family, gifts which would all too soon be needed to support them in exile.

THE ADORATION OF THE MAGI—Giovanni da Fiesole was a Dominican monk in Florence who eventually became the prior of the Dominican convent there. In a time when artists fought furiously over rich commissions and public acclaim, this painter was so beloved that he became affectionately known as Fra Angelico, or Brother Angel. His contemporaries considered his saintliness to be so genuine that they said he never painted the Crucifixion without weeping and never picked up his brush without a prayer.

Fra Angelico learned his art as a painter of illuminations in manuscripts. Illuminators gave loving attention to miniscule detail, worked in rich colors and gold leaf, and learned how to create an inner light within their tiny frame. They used the richness and contrast of color itself to create a sense of depth.

Fra Angelico collaborated with a Carmelite monk, Fra Filippo Lippi, on his masterful The Adoration of the Magi. The painting radiates a golden hue, befitting the birth of a royal child. The monk-artists, in sumptious detail and color, show the Magi at the feet of Jesus and his mother. They have approached from the ruined gate at the left, followed by a large entourage of curious travelers and townsfolk. Word of this startling visit to tiny Bethlehem spreads up the hill on the right, as townspeople collect and gawk. Ever mindful of Jesus' profound commitment to social justice and the needs of the poor, Fra Angelico shows representatives of the underprivileged and maimed, the deranged and outcast, watching from afar.

Mary is regal and serene in the presence of these noble visitors, but she has, after all, known the angel of the Most High God and been visited by the Holy Spirit of God. Fra Angelico portrays the infant with a sense of developed personhood unusual for so young a child. By this means, the artist suggests the divine nature of the child.

THE ADORATION OF THE MAGI
Fra Angelico (Florentine, active 1417-1455); Fra Filippo Lippi (Florentine, c. 1406-1469); Painting on wood;
Diameter 137.2 cm. (53.5 in.); Samuel H. Kress Collection 1952

ADORATION OF THE MAGI
Sandro Botticelli (Florentine, 1444/45-1510); Painting on wood; 70.2 x 104.2 cm. (27.4 x 40.6 in.);
Andrew W. Mellon Collection 1937

30

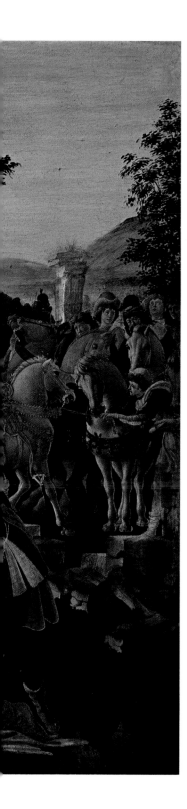

ADORATION OF THE MAGI—Alessandro di Mariano Filipepi, better known as Botticelli or "little barrel," was probably a student of Fra Filippo Lippi. He painted for members of the Medici family, including Lorenzo the Magnificent; he also worked on frescoes for the Sistine Chapel. During his later years he came under the influence of the fiery religious reformer Savonarola and became concerned with purifying the church and its faith.

Botticelli is best known for his classical themes and idealized subjects. He rhythmically balances line, rich color, and planar composition to place his subject spatially in harmony with the background. He sifts through to the essence of truth in his scene, and ponders it in peaceful reflection rather than in dynamic action.

In The Adoration of the Magi, Mary and the infant Jesus are the focus not only of the people but also of all the internal perspective provided by the buildings. The recurrent reds and blues in the worshipers' garments are combined in Mary's costume, drawing attention again to her and to the child. Mary is idealized perfection, very like Botticelli's secular version of the female ideal in another masterpiece, *The Birth of Venus*. For this artist there is little differentiation between the secular and the religious. As a Florentine painter, Botticelli sets his idyllic scene in the Tuscan hills, capturing the translucent atmosphere as well as the dark greens of the vicinity.

The faces of many Medici family members and retainers appear among the Magi and their entourage. There is a sense of melancholy in their visage and demeanor which presages Jesus' Passion. They possess a blend of calm nobility and alert eagerness, while the Virgin is a center of reflective contemplation in this scene charged with brooding energy.

THE FLIGHT INTO EGYPT
Vittore Carpaccio (Venetian, c. 1460/65-1523/26); Painting on wood; 72.0 x 111.5 cm. (28.1 x 43.5 in.);
Andrew W. Mellon Collection 1937

The Flight into Egypt

Reminiscent of the way he had revealed himself to the patriarchs of old, God now spoke to the Magi and to Joseph in dreams. He warned the Magi not to return to Herod, but to leave secretly for their own country by a different road. That night the Magi disappeared as mysteriously as they had appeared.

Meanwhile, God warned Joseph to flee at once from Herod's country with Mary and the infant Jesus, and to take them to the safety of Egypt until Herod was dead. Quickly gathering their few belongings, the Holy Family hurried off into the night toward Egypt. We do not know how they traveled nor which route they followed across the harsh Sinai to the Nile. We can only surmise that with the gifts of the Magi they were able to soften the hardship of their journey.

During the centuries following the exodus of the Children of Israel under Moses from Egypt, the two peoples had settled into peaceful relationships. Eventually a growing number of Jews moved to Egypt, setting up their businesses and schools. Indeed, Alexandria had become one of the foremost centers of Jewish learning. We do not know whether Joseph and Mary had relatives among the large Jewish communities of Alexandria or Heliopolis, but they certainly could have found a safe haven there. Joseph could well have set himself up as a carpenter while the Holy Family awaited the time when Herod would no longer be a threat.

THE FLIGHT INTO EGYPT—Vittore Carpaccio was a prolific Venetian painter who often undertook commissions for the doge as well as for various churches and noble clients. His paintings wonderfully capture the essence of the luminous Venetian atmosphere. Carpaccio uses the sky as a sparkling mantle to envelop his landscape.

There is a dreamy quality to The Flight into Egypt. Instead of revealing the frantic urgency of a sudden escape from certain death, Carpaccio demostrates the serene confidence of Mary and Joseph, and even the donkey, that they are protected by the omnipotent hand of God. They move tranquilly and surely through a peaceful countryside, sheltered from danger or want by the Lord. Joseph walks in a lush, colorful border along the path, leading the donkey. The donkey's bearing is both regal and gentle, as though it senses the importance of the mother and child it carries. They, in turn, sit on the donkey's back as though it were a throne; only Joseph seems to be a part of the everyday working world.

In the distance a Venetian gondola moves slowly upstream toward a Venetian-style footbridge just beyond the junction of a tributary. Even if those in the boat noticed the family on the road, little would they sense the urgency of that steady journey toward the distant land of Egypt.

THE REST ON THE FLIGHT INTO EGYPT— The earliest mention of Gerard David is in 1484, when records show he was admitted into the painters' guild in Bruges. He was of the Flemish school and learned some of his skills from the great van Eyck brothers. David's career met with much success and he received many municipal and ecclesiastical commissions.

In The Rest on the Flight into Egypt, David shows Joseph in the background foraging for food during the tiring journey. The countryside is similar to the rolling hills of the southern Netherlands near the Belgium border. Fifteenth century houses and villages lie in the distance. While Joseph knocks chestnuts from a tree, and the saddled donkey waits patiently for the next leg of the journey, Mary helps the young boy Jesus to eat some grapes. These are a traditional symbol of Jesus' death, memorialized in the wine of the Last Supper. The scene is tranquil, filled with both tenderness and a high seriousness. The manner in which Mary holds the grape cluster as she caresses Jesus reveals David's characteristic refinement. Even in the midst of hasty flight for survival, Mary and the boy show controlled emotion as they listen to Joseph's efforts off in the distance.

THE REST ON THE FLIGHT INTO EGYPT
Gerard David (Flemish c. 1460-1523); Painting on wood; 45.0 x 44.5 cm. (17.6 x 17.4 in.); Andrew W. Mellon Collection 1937

The Massacre of the Innocents

When the Magi failed to return to Herod's court, Herod acted swiftly and decisively to rid himself of a possible rival. He ordered his troops to raid Bethlehem and slay any male child they could find who was two years old or younger. It was Herod's intention thereby to include "the newborn king" in the massacre of children.

Without warning and with ruthless efficiency Herod's troops carried out their orders, leaving a trail of terror and lifelong emptiness among the families of Bethlehem. The shrill keening of heartbroken mothers could be heard throughout the town.

For Herod's horror-hardened troops this was but another bloody assignment to be undertaken. Herod had even ordered the murder of his wife and some of his children, not to mention the nobles he had killed in order to acquire their property and wealth, or the religious leaders whom he had burned alive for disagreeing with him.

THE MASSACRE OF THE INNO-CENTS—Jacques Callot was a French engraver and etcher who worked during the early seventeenth century, making his home in Nancy. He had been apprenticed to a silversmith who also did engraving. Callot adapted a varnish used by French lute makers to the engraving process, and thereby created the method of etching with exceedingly fine lines. He was the most skillful etcher of his time, and to this day few have exceeded his ability.

Callot's most famous series of etchings were done for the Spanish vice-regent of the Netherlands, showing the Spanish capture of the town of Breda in 1625. These prints so impressed the French king that he commissioned a similar series of etchings of his own victories. Living at a time when prolonged war decimated populations and destroyed commerce and agriculture, Callot reflects in The Massacre of the Innocents the all-too-common seventeenth-century experience of soldiers ravaging a town.

Callot shows the massacre occurring in a grandiose Baroque city similar to those national capitals being built in Europe in his day. The disproportion in scale between Herod's huge palace and the small human figures underlines the impersonal cruelty of this act, ordered for "reasons of state." Ermine-robed Herod the Great sits on a throne on the balcony surrounded by fawning courtiers. He watches the blood-soaked scene in the plaza far below. Soldiers seize young boys from their hysterical mothers, stabbing, strangling, and dashing tiny bodies to the pavement. On the edge of the far balcony a soldier is about to drop an infant to the ground. Officers direct the slaughter, as they rush back and forth on their mounts shouting instructions to the troops. One can almost hear the wailing of the women, the terrified cries of the children, and the harsh oaths of the soldiers as they pursue their grisly task.

THE MASSACRE OF THE INNOCENTS
Jacques Callot (French, 1592-1635); Etching; 13.7 x 10.7 cm. (5.3 x 4.2 in.);
Rudolph L. Baumfeld Collection

Childhood

Following the narratives concerning his infancy, there is no information about Jesus' childhood, adolescence, and young adulthood apart from the vignette which describes his visit to the Temple when he was twelve. One can only surmise that the patterns of his childhood were similar to those of other Jewish children of that time.

We can imagine Mary nourishing the infant Jesus at her own breast, deepening the bond which usually exists between a mother and her firstborn son. We can visualize her delighting in his first steps, comforting him when he fell down and bruised himself, teaching him to feed himself, and praying over him when she put him to bed at night. On the Sabbath, no doubt, he watched her light the candles at the family table and learned the haunting words of the Shema: "Hear, O Israel: The Lord our God is one Lord. And thou shalt love the Lord thy God with all thine heart, and with all thy soul, and with all thy might."

Joseph must have taught young Jesus to use a saw, a plane, and a hammer—tools of an honorable trade. He doubtless took the boy to the synagogue, the center of Jewish teaching in Nazareth; there Jesus would have learned the history of his people, from the call of Abraham through the bondage in Egypt, the exile, and return. He would have been taught about the glories of King David, his own ancestor, and he would have learned to read from the scrolls in the tabernacle. Jesus was such an apt pupil that in years to come scholars in Jerusalem would marvel at his astuteness whenever they encountered him.

As a young boy Jesus played on the hills surrounding Nazareth and looked down on the broad sweep of the Plain of Esdraelon. In his mind's eye he could see the infantry of Deborah and Barak clashing with the Canaanite chariots. He could also envision the tragic death of King Saul following the defeat of his troops by the Philistines at Gilboa. He might have visited the site of Solomon's fortress at Megiddo, from which patrols had kept peace in the land.

Although Nazareth was tiny and remote, it lay beside the path of world history. Jesus' intense feeling for the interplay between God's purposes and the events of history was born in his devout Jewish home, nurtured in his synagogue education, and matured as he pondered all that had happened in the land that spread out before him.

The tenderness and supportive love that Jesus knew is often idealized in the art that portrays Mary and her child.

MADONNA AND CHILD
Giotto di Bondone (Florentine, c. 1266-1337); Painting on wood; 85.5 x 62.0 cm. (33.3 x 24.2 in.); Samuel H. Kress Collection 1937

MADONNA AND CHILD—Giotto di Bondone stands as a giant among his contemporaries. He was an architect and sculptor as well as a painter. His sense of the three-dimensional solidity of objects in space turned the course of painting away from the single-plane icons of Late Antique and Byzantine art toward a natural portrayal of living people. Giotto's art was the initial embodiment of the new spirit which came to be called the Renaissance.

In the lovely Madonna and Child, Giotto's debt to the centuries-long tradition of Byzantine icons can be clearly seen. The poses of mother and child, details of dress, and the use of gold leaf to provide a nonspatial, timeless background are all elements of Byzantine style. But Giotto makes *this* Madonna and *this* Child come alive in a new way by giving them a sculptural weight which suggests real, immediate presence. Similarly, where in the earlier tradition of icons the faces of mother and child were generally stylized and without individual personality, Giotto here gives his Madonna and Child that psychological depth and individuality which would characterize the new movement in artistic freedom.

MADONNA AND CHILD—Artists of the early fifteenth century experimented in three dimensions in sculpture and terra-cotta modeling; they tried as well to give three-dimensional effects to their paintings by using systems of perspective and shading.

This terra-cotta figure of the Madonna and Child stands nearly four feet tall and is richly painted and gilded. Here the artist shows a passive, but observant, Jesus held by Mary on her left hip in the time-honored way of all mothers. Rolls of baby fat speak of good nourishment and robust health.

Mary smiles with a kind of inner vision, the only indication in this figure that there may be more than meets the eye. The child confidently entrusts himself to his mother; his thumb in his mouth is the only indication of self-awareness as he gazes placidly at the viewer. This sculpture is a timeless expression of the relationship between mother and child, most appropriate for portraying Mary and Jesus in his first year of life.

MADONNA AND CHILD
Florentine School (c. 1425); Terra-cotta
sculpture, painted and guilded; H. 122.0 cm.
(47.6 in.); Andrew W. Mellon Collection 1937

THE ALBA MADONNA—Raphael was a somewhat younger contemporary of the great Michelangelo and a popular rival for commissions and fame. He was from Urbino and worked extensively in Rome and throughout Italy. This famous Madonna and Child was painted for the influential family of Alba.

Using a characteristic circular format, the artist shows the mother and child with their young cousin John, later to be called John the Baptist. The youthful John, already dressed in rough skins, looks up at the cross the infant Jesus holds in his outstretched hand. John embraces the foot of the cross, symbolizing his own early death for the Kingdom he proclaimed. Mary, too, gazes at the cross, pondering its hard reality in her

THE ALBA MADONNA
Raphael (Umbrian, 1483-1520); Painting transferred from wood to canvas;
Diameter 94.5 cm. (36.9 in.); Andrew W. Mellon Collection 1937

own life. John seems troubled and earnest; Mary appears serene and almost transfigured. Jesus is the source of energy in this picture; both John and Mary are responsive to his initiative. He holds up the cross as a symbol of his own journey, yet looks beyond it in hope and trust.

THE MADONNA OF HUMILITY
*Fra Angelico (Florentine, c. 1417-1455); Painting on wood; 61.0 x 45.5 cm.
(23.8 x 17.7 in.); Andrew W. Mellon Collection 1937*

THE MADONNA OF HUMILITY—In this rich panel Fra Angelico shows the Virgin adoring the Christ Child on her lap. Two angels support a cloth-of-gold arras or drapery behind her, as for a queen. But Mary, in token of her humility, sits on a cushion on the ground rather than on a royal throne. Her halo bears the traditional Latin translation of words spoken to her by Gabriel at the time of the annunciation, "Hail, Mary, full of grace!"

Delicate and elegant, in any other circumstance Mary would be one to whom homage is paid. Yet here she crosses her arms in reverence before her son, her long fingers tapering gracefully toward her shoulders. With her perfect poise this Mary is not the wife of a work-gnarled craftsman, but the daughter of a Florentine banker seen in the private quarters of a Renaissance palazzo. Even the angels remind one of discreet, loyal servants who protect her moment of private reflection.

Jesus is displayed with Mary as his backdrop. While his position is physically impossible, the juxtaposition of these two independent figures on perpendicular planes is artistically satisfying. The child exists on his own, with little sense of dependence on his mother in this painting. It is hard to imagine this idealized child crying, needing cleaning, or hurting himself and running to his mother for comfort. Mary, however, is wholly absorbed in contemplation of the child. She loves and adores him, the angels adore her for doing so, and we the viewers are also admitted to this circle of intimate worship.

MADONNA AND CHILD—Son of an accomplished goldsmith, Albrecht Dürer worked out of his studio in Nurnberg. During the late fifteenth and early sixteenth centuries Dürer was a main intermediary between the still Gothic art of Northern Europe and the flourishing new visual culture of the Italian Renaissance. He seems to be alone in his ability to translate the innovations of the South into works which could be understood by his Northern colleagues. He combined an Italian monumentality and drama with the nervous energy and love of detail of his German and Flemish forebears.

In his Madonna and Child, Dürer adapts an Italian model to his obviously German figures, who are blond and pink-skinned. The child is blue-eyed; the Madonna has vibrant amber eyes. Both are full-boned, well-fleshed, tulip-lipped; it is not difficult to imagine meeting them in towns along the Rhine today. The child has an integrity of his own as he looks out with penetrating vision to a mission only he can see. The Madonna bears the responsibility of this child with sobriety and determination, a heavy burden for so young a woman.

Beyond the window the life of the world goes on. Travelers, knights, and castle dwellers pursue their routines unaware of the destiny shared by the young woman and her child.

MADONNA AND CHILD
*Albrecht Dürer (German, 1471-1528); Painting on wood; 50.2 x 39.7 cm. (19.6 x 15.5 in.);
Samuel H. Kress Collection 1952*

Jesus Visits Jerusalem, Age Twelve

The Temple in Jerusalem played a central role throughout the life of Jesus. His parents took him there to be presented and redeemed when he was an infant. As an adult he often sought its sacred environs to celebrate the annual cycle of religious festivals. In a moment of righteous indignation he cleansed the Temple from commercial exploitation. And ultimately he was condemned to death by the Sanhedrin on the allegation that he had blasphemed the Temple.

It is altogether appropriate that the only glimpse of Jesus' boyhood is a brief account of his visit to the Temple with his parents when he was twelve. It was customary for pious Jewish men to visit the Temple several times during the year for the various feasts and celebrations. One can assume that Joseph, as a devout man, went whenever possible to the Temple and took the young boy with him. Women attended the festivals less often, but tried not to miss the most significant of the annual religious festivals, the Passover.

When Jesus was twelve, his parents took him to Jerusalem for the Passover. At the end of the festival Joseph and Mary started back to Nazareth with their relatives and friends. They had gone several miles before they noticed that Jesus was missing. After returning to Jerusalem and searching frantically for three days in every place they could think of, they finally found him in the Temple, quietly discussing the meaning of God's law with scholars and religious leaders. When his parents reprimanded him for the worry he had caused them, Jesus replied that it was only natural that he should be in "his Father's house" and engaged in "his Father's business."

CHRIST AMONG THE DOCTORS—A retable is a large screen behind an altar, usually with many panels. It became a regular practice to decorate the panels with scenes from the Bible and from the lives of the saints. Sometimes the scenes were ornately carved from wood; sometimes they were painted.

The "Reyes Católicos" were Isabella of Castile and Ferdinand of Aragon, whose marriage helped create Spanish unity in the fifteenth century. Under their rule the Spanish forces expelled the Moors, and Spain became a single Catholic state.

Isabella and Ferdinand commissioned this magnificent retable on the occasion of the marriage of their daughter. It was painted by an anonymous artist known to us only as the Master of the Retable of the Reyes Católicos. One of the panels shows Christ Among the Doctors. Jesus is seated magisterially in the place of authority. He is delineating a fine point of dogma. The learned authorities try to follow his argument, referring to their sources for further enlightenment and enumerating their points of disputation on their fingers. They do not appear antagonistic to being instructed by so young a mentor, but careful and thoughtful as they consider a new insight. This is a disturbing experience for them.

Mary and Joseph stand at the entrance, having just located Jesus after their long search. Mary is astounded by what she sees, and responds with awe and adoration. Joseph is less sensitive to the meaning of what has happened; he seems anxious to get back to his work in Nazareth, and points impatiently toward the boy.

Although this retable was painted in Spain for the Spanish rulers, the style is Flemish. The buildings seen through the open door and the architectural detail and perspective are typical of Flanders in the fifteenth century. Nevertheless, the proud faces are thoroughly Spanish and aristocratic.

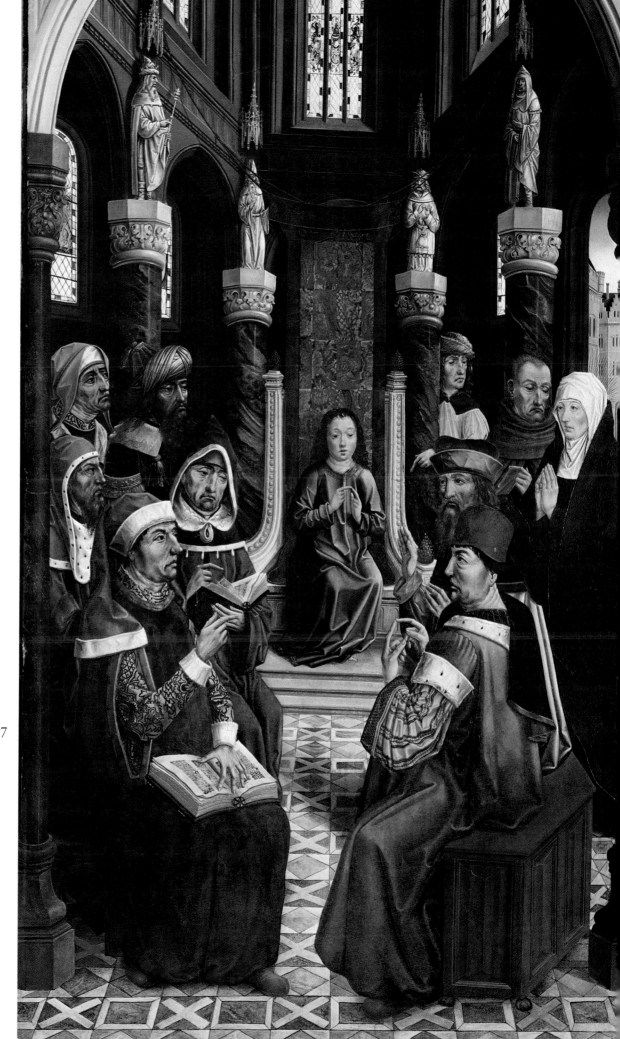

CHRIST AMONG
THE DOCTORS
*Master of the Retable of the
Reyes Católicos;
(Hispano-Flemish, late XV
Century); Painting on wood;
156.3 x 94.0 cm. (61.0 x 36.7
in.); Samuel H. Kress
Collection 1952*

CHRIST BETWEEN HIS PARENTS, RETURNING FROM THE TEMPLE
Rembrandt van Rijn (Dutch, 1606-1669); Etching; 9.4 x 14.4 cm. (3.7 x 5.6 in.);
Rosenwald Collection

*CHRIST BETWEEN HIS PAR-
ENTS, RETURNING FROM THE
TEMPLE*—Although best known for his
paintings and drawings, Rembrandt also
made nearly 300 etchings. The great majority of these were scenes from the New
Testament.

In Christ Between His Parents, made
in 1654, Rembrandt shows the twelve-
year-old Jesus returning to Nazareth from
Jerusalem with Mary and Joseph. In swift,
expressive lines the artist shows Jesus telling Mary the substance of the discussions
which took place in the Temple, center of
Israel's religious life. The boy is filled with
his subject and shares it wholly and without guile. Mary listens, patiently, lovingly,
wonderingly, but without fully compre-
hending the content or import of what is
being said.

Rembrandt hides Joseph's face in dark
shadow under the brim of a peasant's hat.
He walks silently beside this boy whom he
has raised, yet who is so much a stranger.
This long hundred-mile walk is our last
glimpse of Joseph in the Bible. It is fitting
that we see him as Rembrandt portrayed
him—solid, earthy, caring, supportive,
somewhat over his depth but nevertheless
constant. Whereas Jesus grasps Mary's
hand to ensure her attention, Joseph holds
Jesus' hand with steadying, unobtrusive
affection.

THE

INISTRY

SAINT JOHN THE BAPTIST
Giulio Campagnola (Paduan, c. 1482-after 1515); Engraving; 33.2 x 23.5 cm. (12.9 x 9.2 in.);
Rosenwald Collection

48

John the Baptist

When he was a young man, John went out into the wilderness to live in solitude, surviving by eating locusts and the honey of wild bees, found in hollows of dead trees. He wore the rough skins of animals and let his hair grow as a sign of his dedication to God. If his family was disappointed that he did not follow his father as a Temple priest, they must nevertheless have taken comfort in his uncompromising commitment to God.

In the fifteenth year of the reign of Tiberius Caesar, John began his ministry: calling the people of Israel to prepare for the advent of the Kingdom of God. Much of this ministry was conducted along the lower reaches of the Jordan River and in the Judean wilderness west of the Dead Sea. His message, which included scathing judgments against the establishment, was essentially twofold: an announcement that the Kingdom of God was "at hand" and a call for moral and spiritual renewal to prepare oneself to be a citizen of that Kingdom. The sign John used as a symbol of that renewal was public baptism by water, most often in the rapidly flowing waters of the Jordan.

People from all sectors of society responded—farmers, tradesmen, soldiers, and even some religious leaders. Throngs of people came from all parts of the country to hear the message proclaimed by this austere prophet. Their strong response was due not only to the power of his personal magnetism, but also to the people's hunger for spiritual realities, a hunger far deeper than existing religious structures were able to satisfy. Most importantly, John created an atmosphere of expectancy: "Someone is coming! and I—I am only his forerunner!"

SAINT JOHN THE BAPTIST—Giulio Campagnola was a North Italian artist whose work spanned the turn of the sixteenth century. He was one of the first engravers, if not the very first, to use stipple engraving as an independent technique. Note how much of his shading and even some of the less distinct lines are composed of tiny dots. This stipple technique enabled Campagnola to approximate in black and white the effects of color and light, particularly in landscapes, which characterized the glorious paintings of his Venetian contemporaries Giorgione and Titian.

Giulio's John the Baptist is a heroic figure, shown in his early thirties at the height of his ministry. He is a vigorous man, hardened by desert life so his bones show prominently as the strong superstructure of a powerful spirit. In his left hand he holds a bowl, suggesting his role as a baptizer. The "desert" in which Campagnola places his Saint John is, in fact, an idealized but recognizable North Italian valley with a fortified farm and shepherds. This Saint John was designed to speak to the people of the artist's own time and place.

The Baptism of Jesus

One day as John was preaching and baptizing along the banks of the Jordan, his kinsman, Jesus, came and asked to be baptized. John was about six months older than Jesus; their mothers were cousins and close friends. John and Jesus were no doubt well acquainted with each other long before this dramatic meeting in Judea.

John's baptizing symbolized both repentance and preparation for citizenship in the Kingdom of God. As Jesus stood before him, John recognized that here was the only person he had ever met who had no need to repent or to be baptized. If there were to be any baptizing, Jesus should rather baptize the Baptizer! No, insisted Jesus; John must baptize him "to fulfil all righteousness." John pronounced the baptismal formula as he plunged Jesus into the water. When Jesus came up out of the water, the Holy Spirit descended on him in the form of a dove. At the same moment the crowd by the river heard a roaring like thunder, and some heard the words from heaven: "This is my beloved Son, in whom I am well pleased."

THE BAPTISM OF CHRIST—Paris Bordone lived in the sixteenth century, a disciple of the great Titian. He learned well from his master how to blend colors into a pleasing and harmonious whole.

In The Baptism of Christ, Bordone combines Counter Reformation religious sentiment with the mixing of artistic styles typical of mid- and late sixteenth century Venetian art. The baptism is conceived not as a public event but as a deeply private act, witnessed only by the angel who holds Jesus' garment and by the small cherubim surrounding the heavenly light from which the Father will speak. The drama of the opening heavens is extended to the figures in the exaggerated musculature of Jesus and especially John, which Bordone has borrowed from Michelangelo. These stylistic elements do not detract, however, from the inwardness and spiritual depth which the artist gives the main actors in his scene.

THE BAPTISM OF CHRIST
Paris Bordone (Venetian, 1500-1571);
Painting on canvas;
129.5 x 132.0 cm. (50.5 x 51.5 in.);
Widener Collection 1942

THE TEMPTATION OF CHRIST
Christoffel Jegher, after Rubens (Flemish, 1596-1653); Woodcut; 33.7 x 44.2 cm. (13.1 x 17.2 in.); Ailsa Mellon Bruce Fund

The Temptation of Jesus

After his baptism Jesus was led by the Holy Spirit into the wastes of the Judean wilderness for a period of forty days and nights. In solitude he reflected on his calling, fasting while he prayed and meditated. Toward the close of this period he was sorely tempted by Satan to renounce his unique calling.

Satan tempted Jesus to use his powers for his own gratification, a seemingly harmless, even beneficial, exercise of miraculous ability: "Turn these stones into bread and feed yourself after this long fast." He was also tempted to use his powers in a spectacular manner to impress the people: "Jump off the Temple pinnacle and let your angels catch you before you hit the ground; then the people will acclaim you the Son of God." Finally came the temptation to be made king of the kind of kingdom everyone knew well enough and wanted. "Worship me," said Satan, "and the political systems of the world are yours, for they are mine to give if I wish."

Jesus answered each of these temptations to abuse his powers and pervert his Messiahship by quoting the law of God as found in the book of Deuteronomy. He would again meet each of these temptations in different guises throughout his ministry.

THE TEMPTATION OF CHRIST—As one of the century's great painters, Peter Paul Rubens created prints of his works both to advertise them and to increase his income by their sale. Rubens commissioned skilled engravers and woodcut artists to work with him in producing these less expensive versions of his paintings. The Temptation of Christ is such a work. The artist is Christoffel Jegher; his name appears at the bottom right. Jegher worked under the guidance, and for the ultimate benefit, of Rubens whose name as the originator of the design appears at the bottom left.

In this rendition of Rubens' design Jegher depicts the scene from an unusual perspective. We are below the "Mount of Temptation," a rise in the Judean wilderness, looking up at the event. In the foreground there is a twisting serpent, reminiscent of the serpent in the Garden of Eden which served as a symbol of the tempter.

Satan appears as a wily old man who offers stones to be turned into bread to feed the hungering Jesus. His face is masked by a full beard and heavy eyebrows. His body posture is strong, impelling, and suggestive. The Devil is so importunate that it would be difficult to refuse his urging.

Jesus is shown as triumphantly resisting. His body turns away from the tempter, and his arm acts as a buffer to ward off Satan's suggestion. The Rubens-Jegher work suggests that two nearly equal opponents are involved in the temptation scene; it is not merely a pious charade. The grand dimensions of this stirring portrayal reflect the magnitude of Jesus' victory.

THE TEMPTATION OF CHRIST
Juan de Flandes (Hispano-Flemish, active 1496-1519); Painting on wood; 21.0 x 15.8 cm. (8.2 x 6.2 in.); Ailsa Mellon Bruce Fund

THE TEMPTATION OF CHRIST—Juan de Flandes was a Flemish painter who worked at the royal court of Spain during the early sixteenth century. He was commissioned by no less an important patron than Queen Isabella of Castile. Juan de Flandes' work represents the final flowering of Gothic art. Note how every leaf in the trees, each petal of the wildflowers, is carefully delineated, reflecting the Gothic love of minute detail.

This wilderness is a verdant paradise compared with the harsh realities of the Judean desert. Satan appears disguised as a monk, piously telling his beads. The perceptive eye of faith, however, can see he is not what he appears to be. The goat-like beard and horns and the webbed feet are traditional symbols of the Devil. Here he holds out a stone and suggests that Jesus assuage his hunger by turning it into bread. Jesus sees the trick for what it is, and the visitor for who he is. He holds up his hand in rejection of the temptation.

Off in the distance the other two temptations are depicted. On the pinnacle of the Temple in a very Gothic Jerusalem the Devil suggests that Jesus hurl himself to the ground below. High on a cliff in the upper left Satan points to the kingdoms of the world and promises them to Jesus if he will only worship him.

53

The First Disciples

It was after the period of reflection in the wilderness that Jesus, on his way to Galilee, met John the Baptist and a crowd of people by the Jordan. John had been telling his disciples about Jesus, calling him "the Lamb of God which taketh away the sin of the world." He affirmed his conviction that Jesus was the Son of God.

As Jesus came near them, two of John's disciples started to follow him. He turned and asked them what they wanted; they asked where he lived, implying that they wished to go there and join him. Jesus then invited the two disciples to stay with him.

So taken with Jesus were they that one of them, a man named Andrew, decided that his brother, Simon, had to meet this remarkable person. He went to find his brother, and his first words to Simon were, "We have found the Messiah." When Jesus saw Simon, he said that while he was now called Simon, the son of Jona, he would in the future be called Cephas, which was Aramaic for stone or rock. Still later, Simon became known as Peter, which is derived from the Greek word "petros," also meaning stone or rock.

Some time after these initial meetings Jesus returned to Galilee, as did Peter and Andrew. One day as Jesus walked along the shores of Lake Galilee, he saw the two brothers busy casting their nets into the water. They were commercial fishermen, and Lake Galilee was famous for its abundance of fresh-water fish. Jesus and the two brothers had come to know and trust each other and now Jesus needed a few chosen companions to assist him. He called out to Andrew and Peter, "Come ye after me, and I will make you to become fishers of men." Joyfully they left their nets and became close friends and disciples of Jesus.

THE CALLING OF THE APOSTLES PETER AND ANDREW—Duccio was the greatest painter in Siena in the early fourteenth century. Siena flourished as a rival to Florence in the wool trade and banking. Its leaders sought to make it the most beautiful city in Italy, with a graceful cathedral and bell tower, and an imposing commercial exchange. The elegant Byzantine style dominated Sienese religious art, and many of the working artists were, in fact, Greeks. For the decoration of the cathedral and the commercial exchange, however, the Sienese chose one of their own sons, Duccio di Buoninsegna.

Duccio painted a number of scenes from the life of Jesus on wood panels for an altarpiece for the Siena cathedral. In one of these, The Calling of the Apostles Peter and Andrew, he shows Jesus standing by the shore of Lake Galilee calling out to the brothers to leave their fishing nets and become fishers of men. The gold background is a Byzantine characteristic, but Duccio makes it seem like a glowing sky at this pivotal moment in the lives of the two fishermen. He has given life to the three figures, including warm flesh tints and three-dimensional modeling.

The importance of this calling of the disciples is evident to all: Jesus issues the call with compelling intentness; Peter raises his hand, his eyes fixed on Jesus, signaling his characteristic impulsiveness by his readiness to follow at once; by contrast Andrew pensively weighs what it will mean to leave a familiar way of life and enter upon an unknown journey.

THE CALLING OF THE APOSTLES PETER AND ANDREW
Duccio di Buoninsegna (Sienese, active 1278-1318/19); Painting on wood; 43.5 x 46.0 cm. (17.0 x 17.9 in.);
Samuel H. Kress Collection 1939

The Marriage in Cana

In the tiny Galilean hill village of Cana, not far from Nazareth, Jesus' mother went to a wedding feast. Jesus was there with his disciples. During the feast Mary leaned over to Jesus and whispered that their host had run out of wine. This was an embarrassment to the bridal couple, and Mary who wanted everyone to enjoy the feast, was concerned for them. Jesus responded to Mary that his concerns and hers were not the same. Nonetheless, he did what she implicitly asked, helping the newlyweds and, more importantly, giving a sign of his own identity and mission.

Jesus told the servants to fill six stone jars with water. Each jar held about twenty-five gallons, and the water was generally used for the daily ceremonial washing and purification of hands and drinking utensils. When the servants had filled the jars, he told them to draw some off and take it to the master of ceremonies. They did so and it was splendid wine. The master of ceremonies complimented the bridegroom on saving the best wine for the end of the festivities.

Because of this miracle, the first of many to be recorded in the Gospels, the disciples became more aware of the glory of Jesus, and they "believed in him."

THE MARRIAGE AT CANA—In this panel of the retable (see page 42), the artist captures several moments of the story. Jesus is shown blessing the water, transforming it into the finest of wine, while Mary looks on in an attitude of thoughtful adoration. At Jesus' left, our right, the steward tastes the miraculous wine, and still farther to Jesus' left sit the new husband and wife. One of the servants presents to the bride a glass of wine drawn from the water jar. The servants are shown smaller in size, indicating they were socially inferior to the members of the wedding party. One servant points to the jars as if to explain what has just happened.

The artist shows a boisterous party in the far room, where this fine wine is no doubt being enjoyed to the full. High in a balcony musicians play lively wedding songs. The evening will undoubtedly end in great hilarity and teasing when the guests, who by then will have had their fill of wine and food, escort the couple to the marriage chamber.

Gothic painters often embellished their work with symbolic elements, such as the tiny dog under the table, which the artist captures in the act of stealing a crust. Placed near the bridal couple, the dog is a traditional symbol of fidelity. Note also the embroidery of the tablecloth which includes the Latin version of the words spoken by the angel Gabriel to Mary: "Hail, Mary, full of grace." This reference is meant to underline Mary's role as intercessor in the miracle.

Finally, Jesus' sad expression and gesture of blessing suggest another meal where wine is served—the Last Supper. The statue of Moses with the tablets of the Old Covenant, above Jesus' head, is a studied contrast to that "New Covenant in my blood" which Jesus would establish.

THE MARRIAGE AT CANA
The Master of the Retable of the Reyes Catolicos (Hispano-Flemish, late XV Century); Painting on wood; 153.4 x 92.6 cm. (59.8 x 36.1 in.); Samuel H. Kress Collection 1952

Nicodemus Visits Jesus

Jesus' fame began to spread as he taught and healed the common people. Soon he came to the attention of the Sanhedrin, the body of religious authorities who governed the religious life of the nation. The Sanhedrin was composed of the high priest, a number of leading priests, experts in the law, and prominent members of two groups called Pharisees and Sadducees. Some priests were Sadducees, and many experts in the law were Pharisees. The Roman government allowed the Sanhedrin to decide most religious and civil matters, except those relating to public taxes and capital punishment.

A member of the Sanhedrin, a Pharisee named Nicodemus, sought out Jesus one night. It is not known whether he was sent by the Sanhedrin to sound out this new teacher, or whether he came out of personal curiosity; nor is it known whether he chose to come at night in order to have a quiet, private interview, or whether he did not want to be recognized.

Nicodemus opened the interview with an implied, but leading, question, "We know you are a teacher from God." Jesus did not comment on this but instead called for "new birth." Normally a young man Jesus' age would be a respectful learner from the older member of the Sanhedrin. Yet Jesus firmly and politely took control of the conversation.

Nicodemus asked Jesus what he meant. How could a grown person be born a second time? This question provided Jesus with the opportunity to comment on spiritual rebirth. He then spoke of Moses lifting up a bronze serpent in the wilderness to save the people from deadly snakes; this, said Jesus, was a sign of his own being lifted up one day to save the people and provide them eternal life. We do not know how Nicodemus responded to Jesus' teaching; we do know that he later defended Jesus in the Sanhedrin when Jesus was accused of blasphemy.

CHRIST AND NICODEMUS
Master P.G. (German, c. 1550); Bronze plaquette; Diameter 5.3 cm. (2.1 in.);
Samuel H. Kress Collection

CHRIST AND NICODEMUS—This sixteenth century medal by a bronzemaster known to us only as Master P.G. shows Jesus talking with Nicodemus, who had come to see him at night. The darkness is suggested by the burning taper on the table, which the artist has situated at the extreme left of his composition so that the raised, light-catching surfaces of the relief seem to reflect the candle's glow. This pictorial effect is a remarkable achievement in a sculptural medium. A wick-trimmer lies beside the candle stand.

Nicodemus has asked how it is possible for a person to be born a second time. He holds out his hand in searching inquiry for spiritual truth. Jesus leans forward to speak to this receptive seeker; he uses both hands to focus Nicodemus' full attention on the point that the second birth is from above.

The two speak in complete privacy. Nicodemus is a Pharisee and a member of the Sanhedrin. He did not taunt Jesus publicly, as did many other Pharisees and religious leaders; rather he sought out this opportunity to learn from Jesus, for his soul was thirsting for more than it already knew. On his part Jesus recognized genuine hunger for spiritual reality when he encountered it, and gladly spent this time with Nicodemus. That this interview bore fruit is amply borne out by Nicodemus' later acts on behalf of Jesus. The closed door suggests the utter seclusion of this meeting. The only other presence is a sleeping dog, curled up in peaceful contentment while the two men talk quietly into the night.

The Samaritan Woman

As Jesus began to preach and heal, he soon gathered more disciples than John the Baptist. This development aroused the interest of the religious authorities and so to avoid premature conflict with them Jesus left Judea for Galilee. Taking the most direct route led him through Samaria, a region most Jews normally avoided, since the Jews and the Samaritans despised each other.

Near the town of Sychar Jesus sent his disciples ahead to buy some food. Hot and tired, he sat down by a well. According to tradition this well had been

CHRIST AND THE WOMAN OF SAMARIA
American School, c. 1720-1740; Painting on canvas; 52.3 x 67.0 cm. (20.4 x 26.1 in.); Gift of Edgar William and Bernice Chrysler Garbisch 1953

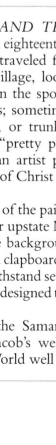

dug by Jacob generations before, and was noted for its sweet, pure water. While he was resting a woman from Sychar came to draw water, and Jesus asked her for a drink. Surprised, she asked how it was that he, a Jew, would deign to speak with a Samaritan woman.

Jesus replied that if she only knew who he was, she would ask *him* for a drink—a drink of living water. She pointed out that he had no bucket to draw water from the well. Where would he get that "living water"? His "water" was new life surging up within the soul, said Jesus. Immediately she asked to be given such water. He bade her call her husband. When she said she was not married, Jesus reminded her that she had had five husbands and was now living with a sixth man, to whom she was not married.

Astounded by his accurate knowledge of her personal life, the woman recognized him to be a prophet. She asked him to resolve for her the long-standing religious difference between Samaritans and Jews, and tell her where she should worship God properly—in Jerusalem, as the Jews said, or on Mount Gerizim as the Samaritans insisted. Neither, said Jesus, for true worship could take place anywhere a person worshiped God "in spirit and in truth." She reminded him that the Messiah would clarify the matter when he came. "I that speak unto thee am he," Jesus replied.

The Samaritan woman ran back to town to tell her friends and neighbors that she had met the Messiah, who had known all about her life. Some came to see for themselves. They asked Jesus to stay with them and teach them. He and his disciples remained in Sychar for two days, and many of the townspeople believed in him.

CHRIST AND THE WOMAN OF SAMARIA—In eighteenth century America itinerant artists traveled from farm to farm and village to village, looking for commissions to paint on the spot. Sometimes they painted portraits; sometimes they decorated furniture, walls, or trunks; and sometimes they painted a "pretty picture" to hang in a room. Such an artist painted this hastily conceived view of Christ and the Woman of Samaria.

The setting of the painting appears to be New England or upstate New York. Sychar, portrayed in the background, is built in the style of northern clapboard or brick buildings which had to withstand severe winters. Their steep roofs were designed to shed heavy snow loads.

Jesus and the Samaritan woman converse beside "Jacob's well," a solidly constructed New World well with pulley, hook, and rope. It appears to be summer, and the trees are in full leaf.

Figure painting was never a strong characteristic of these roving American artists. Mostly self-taught, they lacked the tradition of anatomical precision fostered over centuries by the European masters. Hands were particularly difficult, as can be seen by the woman's right hand, which barely grasps her water jug. The fingers on Jesus' right hand are also out of proportion. The left hand of Jesus and that of the woman are identical, perhaps a pose which the artist found easy to achieve.

For all his crudeness this anonymous artist succeeds in capturing an honest encounter between Jesus and a person who is searching, albeit not fully aware she is searching, for direction in life. Awakened to this search, she will never be the same for having talked with that stranger one day beside the well.

Teaching and Healing

ARISE, TAKE UP THY BED, AND WALK
Jan van Hemessen (Flemish, c. 1500-1566); Painting on wood; 108.0 x 76.0 cm.
(42.1 x 29.6 in.); Gift of Chester Dale 1943

ARISE, TAKE UP THY BED, AND WALK—Jan van Hemessen, a painter of the sixteenth century in Antwerp, was a founder of what has come to be known as "genre" painting—that is, the depiction of subjects taken from everyday life. In the late Renaissance there was a definite order of importance in the subjects which an artist might treat. The most prestigious were those dealing with themes from the Bible or classical Greek and Roman history. Next came portraiture, especially of the great and famous. Lowest on the ladder, indeed hardly respectable at all for serious artists, were genre subjects. Great masters like the Brueghels and van Hemessen dignified genre painting by combining it with religious subjects.

Thus, in Arise, Take Up Thy Bed, and Walk van Hemessen's carefully observed study of the paralytic's bedding, almost a still life in itself, is "acceptable" because it is part of the larger biblical subject. The artist's emphasis on genre detail actually helps communicate the religious point of the story, for the monumental mass of bedding functions as a symbol of the dimensions of the healing.

In the distance the man's four friends are still on the roof of a very Italian villa. One man peers down the hole that they have just made in the tiles. The paralyzed man lies on his pallet on the ground in front of Jesus, who reaches out to tell him that his sins are forgiven and his body healed, The crowd watches. Some scoff, as indicated by their posture showing resistance to what they see and hear. Others believe and marvel. In the foreground the man is seen walking away from that experience, pondering the miracle of his healing and his forgiveness.

CHRIST HEALING THE LEPER—In this pen and wash drawing by an anonymous Dutch artist of the seventeenth century Jesus is shown healing a leper. In the Bible the term "leprosy" may well have referred to any one of the number of diseases characterized by open, running ulcers. The disease came under the proscription of the law, and a leper was considered unclean, an outcast from normal society. His person, his clothing, and his house polluted anyone who came into contact with them. Anyone who touched a leper became unclean.

During his ministry Jesus gladly healed many lepers and told them how to be officially declared clean and returned to society. In Christ Healing the Leper Jesus reaches out his right hand to touch the leper's bandaged head. His eyes are closed, and his left hand is raised in prayer as he pronounces the healing formula.

With a few deft lines, fluid and assured, the artist delineates figures and landscape. His wash shadings give body and depth to the figures.

CHRIST HEALING THE LEPER
Anonymous (Dutch, early XVII Century); Pen and wash drawing; 10.8 x 8.3 cm. (4.2 x 3.2 in.);
Ailsa Mellon Bruce Fund

During three event-filled years Jesus traveled up and down the land, from Mount Hermon in the north to Jerusalem in the south. He taught the people about his Kingdom, about love, about true obedience to God who loved them, and about the life to come. Sometimes he taught in plain words; sometimes in obscure, mysterious parables; and sometimes in direct argument and confrontation with those who disagreed with him. His teaching was so effective, and so memorable, that he was most often addressed as "Teacher."

The common people loved his teachings, for he affirmed their worth. The religious authorities came to hate and fear his teachings, for he struck at the heart of a religious system which seemed to be rooted more in the letter of the law of God than in its spirit. These leaders genuinely believed Jesus was blasphemous in his rejection of what they understood God to demand from a good person.

As he taught, he also healed. He healed both because he felt compassion and because his healing miracles were a sign to the people of his Messiahship. One day some men brought a paralyzed friend to Jesus. Dramatically they tore up the roof of the house in which Jesus was teaching and let their friend down by ropes until he lay in front of Jesus. The crowd was astonished at this behavior, and even more that Jesus forgave the man his sins. The religious teachers in the audience accused Jesus of blaspheming, since only God can forgive sins. But, which was easier, Jesus asked, to forgive sins or to heal the body? Then he ordered the man to take up his bed and walk away—which he did!

Jesus' healings ranged from casting out demons, curing epilepsy and skin diseases, restoring sight and hearing, to raising the dead to life. Everywhere he went the people flocked to him, hoping to be cured themselves or wanting to see with their own eyes some wondrous miracle. Always gentle and supportive of those he healed, Jesus refused to exploit them for his own benefit.

CHRIST PREACHING—In Christ Preaching, Rembrandt shows Jesus standing on a platform preaching to townspeople. He is entirely engrossed in what he is saying, his head tilted slightly to the side and forward. His entire demeanor denotes pensive strength and solidity.

There is a wide and very human range of response among the audience. A woman who has brought her infant and little boy sits straight and listens intently. The child is bored by all these adults and words. He quietly passes the time playing with a ball of string and making designs on the floor with his finger. Next to the woman an old man looks off in the distance as he ponders something Jesus has just said. Against the wall on the right a tired man nods, a sight familiar to all preachers.

It was said that the common people heard Jesus gladly. Surely the man who sits at his feet and the group directly behind him hang on every word. These people are not rich in worldly goods, but the hunger in their faces is for spiritual realities rather than material ones. It was to such people that Jesus said, "I am the bread of life."

CHRIST PREACHING
Rembrandt van Rijn (Dutch, 1606-1669); Etching; 15.5 x 20.7 cm. (6.0 x 8.1 in.); Gift of W. G. Russell Allen

CHRIST, WITH THE SICK AROUND HIM, RECEIVING
LITTLE CHILDREN
*Rembrandt van Rijn (Dutch, 1606-1669); Etching; 27.9 x 39.3 cm. (10.9
x 15.3 in.); Gift of R. Horace Gallatin*

CHRIST, WITH THE SICK AROUND HIM, RE-CEIVING LITTLE CHILDREN—This marvelous etching by Rembrandt is known as "The Hundred Guilder Print," because it once sold for that amount, an unprecedented price for an etching. It is a self-contained drama in which light and shadow underline the range of human feelings represented. In the center, a woman presents her baby to Jesus for blessing. He reaches out toward the child, and we remember Jesus' words about little children: "Of such is the kingdom of heaven." Another mother waits, as her young son tugs at her skirts to pull her to the Master.

To the right the infirm come for healing. A woman lies on her pallet, lost in her inner world of pain and hopelessness. A man tries to attract Jesus' attention to his friend, whom he has brought in a wheelbarrow. Old and young, they plead for help. Some walk, some kneel, some hold themselves up with home made crutches. To Jesus' immediate right some disciples watch what is for them a familiar scene. The bald man is perhaps Peter; the long-haired young man, seated, may be John. The Gospels suggest that many days in Jesus' three-year ministry were much like this one portrayed by Rembrandt.

65

The Death of John the Baptist

John the Baptist continued his preaching and baptizing up and down the reaches of the Jordan. The common people loved him, following him with such enthusiasm that John was regarded as a political threat by Herod Antipas, son of Herod the Great and ruler of Galilee and Perea. The Jewish historian Josephus wrote that Herod imprisoned John in the fortress of Machaerus.

Herod had married the daughter of Aretas IV, king of the Nabateans, but then divorced her to marry Herodias, the wife of his half-brother, Herod Philip. John publicly condemned Herod for this unlawful relationship and, in doing so, aroused the unquenchable hatred of Herodias. Although, according to the Jewish historian Josephus,

Herod placed John in prison to avert a possible revolt, Herod was actually of two minds about John. In fact, he heard John often in personal audiences, and even allowed John's disciples to visit him.

After he had imprisoned John, Herod gave a feast for the chief members of his court and leading landowners of Galilee. It was his birthday, and when everyone was well wined and dined, Herodias' daughter Salome danced for them. Herod was so taken with her that he impulsively promised her anything she wanted, "unto the half of my kingdom." Salome sought her mother's advice, whereupon Herodias told her to ask for the head of John the Baptist. Herod could not back down in front of his guests, however much he may have wanted to. So, reluctantly he ordered John's head served to Salome on a large platter. Salome in turn presented it to her mother, who must have gloated long and triumphantly over the grisly gift.

Herod later released John's body to his disciples, and they placed it in a tomb. Some of them went to tell Jesus what had happened.

THE BEHEADING OF JOHN THE BAPTIST
Rembrandt van Rijn (Dutch, 1606-1669); Etching; 15.7 x 12.4 cm. (6.1 x 4.8 in.); Ailsa Mellon Bruce Fund

THE BEHEADING OF JOHN THE BAPTIST—As always, Rembrandt captures a very human moment in his depiction of a scene. The executioner is in the act of sheathing his sword after severing John's head from his body. Doubtless the corpse was still twitching and blood still pouring from the torn arteries. The executioner has calmly wiped his sword clean, and now returns it to its scabbard, focusing all his attention on the routine care of his weapon. John was nothing to him—nor is death itself, a common enough occurrence for one in the service of Herod Antipas.

Most of John's body lies in the shadow, forcing us to stare at the blindfolded head lying by itself in terrifying isolation. In the distance three members of Herod's court watch through a rough window in the stone wall, their faces showing the shock of having witnessed John's violent end.

When the executioner finishes sheathing his sword, he will pick up John's head, set it on the large platter at the foot of the stairs, and bear it to the king in the banquet hall above.

THE DANCE OF SALOME—
Benozzo Gozzoli was a popular painter of the early Italian Renaissance. He worked on some commissions with Fra Angelico and was greatly influenced by the older master.

In The Dance of Salome, Gozzoli shows the story in a kind of unitary triptych. To the right, the young woman dances at the birthday party of her stepfather. Herod, with the ermine-trimmed cape, is surrounded by courtiers. He holds his heart, suggesting he has been ravished by the beauty and sexual force of this graceful girl. His eyes burn with controlled lust as he promises her up to half of his kingdom. The counselor to his right shows concern about managing this unpredictable old lecher, whereas the courtier on his left, like the king, is absorbed in the dance.

Against the wall three young servants roll their eyes in sham disbelief of this latest of Herod's scandals. Next to them Herodias stands with folded arms and a distant gaze, betraying her disgust at her husband's behavior.

Nevertheless, Herodias was opportunistic enough not to let her disgust interfere with her hatred of John the Baptist. At her instruction Salome asks for John's head. To the left, the executioner readies himself for his gruesome task.

Finally, in a recessed chamber adjacent to the banquet hall, Salome kneels before her mother as she presents John's head on a platter. Herodias gazes on her trophy with disdainful triumph. At last she has had her way over Herod's objections to killing the Baptist.

THE DANCE OF SALOME
*Benozzo Gozzoli (Florentine, 1420-1497); Painting on wood; 23.8 x 34.3 cm. (9.3 x 13.4 in.);
Samuel H. Kress Collection 1952*

Jesus Walks on Water

After Jesus had fed the five thousand along the shore of Lake Galilee, he sent his disciples by boat to an appointed place farther down the lake. He remained to give his final words to the crowd, and then went up to the nearby hills for a period of meditation and prayer.

During the night a strong wind built up, turning the peaceful lake into a churning sea. Even though manned by experienced fishermen, the boat was pushed back toward the center of the lake and was in danger of being swamped. Sometime in the early hours of the morning, Jesus looked out from the hills and saw the boat tossed by wave and wind. He went to join his disciples—and he walked upon the water.

Probably Jesus meant only to reassure them of his protective care, for he seemed to be walking past them to the appointed meeting place. At first they thought they saw a ghost, but Jesus assured them it was he. When Peter saw that Jesus did not intend to enter the boat, with characteristic impulsiveness he called out, "Bid me come unto thee on the water." "Come!" Jesus said. Filled with faith, Peter took a step from the boat onto the water. But once he felt the fury of the gale, his faith failed him, and he started to sink. "Lord, save me!" he cried out. Jesus reached out his hand, grabbed the sinking Peter, and with the other disciples' help heaved him into the boat. Then he got in himself. At once the winds stopped blowing and the waters quieted down. Astonished that Jesus had such power over the violent forces of nature, the disciples fell to their knees before him and said, "Of a truth thou art the Son of God." They then continued across the lake to the region of Gennesaret, where Jesus again took up his teaching and healing.

JESUS AND SAINT PETER ON THE WATER
Jacques Callot (French, 1592-1635); Engraving; 11.5 x 7.5 cm. (4.5 x 2.9 in.);
Rudolph L. Baumfeld Collection

JESUS AND SAINT PETER ON THE WATER—In this engraving of Jesus and Saint Peter on the Water the artist shows Jesus as giver of life in the midst of threatening death. Overloaded and with little freeboard, the disciples' boat is in heavy seas and sure to be swamped. The likely fate of the crew is suggested by Callot in the hollow, staring eyes which are like sockets in their skulls.

Turbulent storm clouds gather overhead as Jesus stretches out his hand to grasp the sinking disciple. Peter's full attention is on Jesus. Terror has been replaced by complete trust as he feels the power of Jesus' authority over nature. Jesus stands firm and secure on top of the water and looks piercingly into Peter's eyes, chiding him for his little faith.

In the background the waters are already beginning to calm. Heaven's angels watch—some with wings, some without; some are young adults, others are children, reflecting the ancient tradition that heaven is populated by a hierarchy of beings ranged in "choirs" from archangels to cherubim.

The Transfiguration

It was while Jesus and his disciples were in Caesarea Philippi that Peter confessed his belief in Jesus as the Messiah. Immediately Jesus began to teach his disciples openly that he would soon suffer, and that this suffering was necessary for him to inaugurate his long-promised Kingdom. A week later he took Peter, James, and John with him onto a high mountain. Tradition holds that this mountain was Mount Tabor, near Nazareth, but it may more likely have been Mount Hermon, not far from Caesarea.

While the three disciples struggled against sleep, Jesus was transformed, or changed in appearance, before their eyes. He seemed to radiate an inner light. Two men appeared with him, also alive with light—Moses and Elijah, representing the law and the prophets from Israel's earlier history. The three luminous figures talked together about Jesus' imminent death in Jerusalem. After Moses and Elijah had vanished, Peter suggested that three tabernacles be put up there and then to commemorate this marvelous event. Suddenly they were surrounded by a cloud, and from within this cloud the disciples heard a voice say, "This is my beloved Son: hear him."

The disciples were filled with an overwhelming mixture of fear and joy. Jesus insisted that they tell no one what they had seen; and as the morning light broke, they returned down the mountain to the ordinary circumstances of life.

THE TRANSFIGURATION—Camillo Procaccini was an engraver in Northern Italy during the late sixteenth and early seventeenth centuries. His native Lombardy was ruled by the Spanish Hapsburgs, and the effect of the Catholic Counter Reformation on artistic expression was at its height. These influences issued in a style known as "Baroque," characterized by theatricality, the portrayal of spiritual ecstacy in terms of intense human emotion, distortions of restrained classical models, and a sense of movement amounting at times to agitation.

Procaccini's The Transfiguration is thoroughly Baroque. Jesus is shown flanked by Moses and Elijah. Moses, on the left, holds the books of the law. Jesus stands on the Mount of Transfiguration, but the two heavenly visitors float in air as the three of them discuss the forthcoming events in Jerusalem. In the foreground Peter, James, and John watch with fear and wonder. Peter is the central figure with his pointing finger.

By alternating areas of bold lines, cross-hatching, and stippling with empty spaces, Procaccini shows Jesus radiant with light and the three disciples emerging from darkness into this light. Jesus looks up into heaven, as though listening to the words from the cloud, "This is my beloved Son."

THE TRANSFIGURATION
Camillo Procaccini (Italian, 1546-1626); Etching; 56.8 x 34.2 cm.
(22.2 x 13.3 in.); Ailsa Mellon Bruce Fund

Camillo procacino
Inle. Inci.

The Woman Taken in Adultery

One morning as Jesus was teaching the people in the Temple courtyard, some of the religious leaders forceably brought a woman through the crowd and stood her before Jesus. They told him that this woman had been seized because she was guilty of adultery. She deserved death by stoning, according to their interpretation of the law. They hoped Jesus might say something they could use in bringing charges against him. Would his known sympathy for sinners put him in conflict with the Mosaic law?

Knowing their intention, Jesus did not fall into their trap. Rather, he turned the situation around. He squatted down on his heels and, without a word, wrote on the ground with his finger. They

CHRIST AND THE WOMAN TAKEN IN ADULTERY—In this large, intricately woven wall hanging the artisans show the adulteress being brought before Jesus for judgment. The woman kneels before Jesus, ashamed, withdrawn, and perhaps fatalistic. She tries to take as little space as possible; she would disappear if she could. Her accusers stand arrogantly and self-righteously around her. They hold stones in their hands, ready to send her to her death.

On either side of the tapestry the four Evangelists are represented with their identifying symbols: from left to right, Saint Mark with a lion; Saint John with an eagle; Saint Matthew with an angel; and Saint Luke with an ox.

The would-be executioners are pillars of society. The townspeople, men and women, hover in the background to gossip and add their encouragement to the leaders in ridding the community of this woman.

Jesus has just spoken the words bidding the one who is without sin to cast the first stone. Suddenly eyes are raised, unfocused, in thought, and hands rise unconsciously as though to ward off some unexpected foe. It is an uncomfortable moment, and soon these people will quietly walk away, one by one, leaving only Jesus and the woman.

Although a single tapestry was woven by scores of people, usually women and young girls, the work followed a designed "cartoon," or drawing, by a single artist. The designer of this tapestry is unknown, as is so often the case. This artist was probably Flemish, working in the early years of the sixteenth century. He has placed the event in a great house, in contrast with the Gospel account, which placed it out-of-doors where Jesus could write on the ground with his finger.

Antwerp, the capital of Flemish tapestry-making, was also an early center for lens grinding. Note the Evangelist on the right, Saint Matthew, wearing a pair of glasses as he listens to his accompanying angel. The Evangelist on the left, Saint Mark, has a forked beard, in the style of late medieval Jewish scholars of the Low Countries.

CHRIST AND THE WOMAN TAKEN IN ADULTERY
Unknown (Flemish, XVI Century); Tapestry; 256.5 x 335.3 cm. (100.0 x 130.8 in.);
Widener Collection 1942

continued to press him for his judgment, stridently repeating that the law called for her execution. He stood up and looked them in the eye as he said, "He that is without sin among you, let him first cast a stone at her." He stooped down again and continued looking at the ground and writing with his finger. One at a time the men walked away, until only Jesus and the woman were left.

What happened to her accusers? he asked the woman. Was there no man left to accuse her? "No man, Lord," she said. He replied that neither did he accuse her. With a tender blend of searching penetration and compassion Jesus told her, "Go, and sin no more." Thus, he treated her as a person of unique value, even though she was presented to him as a "case" which called for judgment. And he dealt with her accusers as men of conscience, even though they came to him as self-righteous executioners.

The Raising of Lazarus

Because of growing opposition of the religious authorities, Jesus withdrew to the east of the Jordan River. There he received a message that Lazarus, his friend and the brother of his good friends Mary and Martha, was very sick. Rather than rushing to their home in Bethany, Jesus remained where he was for another two days. He then traveled at leisure to Bethany, where he found Lazarus had died four days earlier.

First Martha, and then Mary, came to meet Jesus as he approached their house. In their grief each of them chided Jesus for not coming earlier to heal Lazarus. Jesus comforted the sisters, stating that *he* was the resurrection and the life, that he alone gave victory over death. Seeing their sorrow at the loss of their brother and their blindness regarding his mission, Jesus wept and groaned in his spirit; he was about to enter into conflict with death itself to prove to all that he could give life.

Jesus asked to be taken to Lazarus' tomb. As he stood before the tomb, he groaned again in the intensity of his struggle with death. A large crowd had gathered to mourn with the sisters. There was much speculation as to Jesus' ability or even willingness to have healed Lazarus. Suddenly Jesus cried out with a loud voice and ordered the stone to be rolled away from the entrance to the tomb. Martha, always the practical one, protested that decomposition of her brother's body would have begun and that the stench would be unbearable. Jesus insisted. Then he cried out again in a loud voice, "Lazarus, come forth!"

As the sisters and the crowd watched breathlessly, the eerie shape of a man wrapped in burial clothes could be seen walking toward them from the dark recesses of the tomb. Even his face was

THE RAISING OF LAZARUS—Lucas van Leyden worked in Antwerp as an engraver during the first half of the sixteenth century. Although he did some painting, van Leyden preferred engraving and is known for very fine and tightly spaced lines. He developed the ability to suggest air-filled space through heavy strokes in the foreground and lighter strokes for objects in the background. Note how he achieves this effect in The Raising of Lazarus.

In earlier works, like this etching, van Leyden was concerned with realism. He fills his scene with human figures. Twelve people crowd his foreground; Lazarus, Peter, and Jesus occupy the center stage. Peter unties the bonds around Lazarus's wrists. A cringing, almost abject, Lazarus kneels before Jesus.

Mary and Martha are in positions of awe and adoration. Some of the curious crowd hang on trees to see what is happening. A religious leader watches from the left, while another comes trudging up the hill from the distant city of Jerusalem accompanied by his servant. Far down the hill other people are on their way to find out what happened here at this tomb near Bethany.

THE RAISING OF LAZARUS
Lucas van Leyden (Dutch, 1494-1533);
Engraving;
28.6 x 20.9 cm. (11.2 x 8.2 in.);
Rosenwald Collection

shrouded. Jesus bade some of the people to loose Lazarus from his wrappings and free him from his death clothes.

The dramatic raising of Lazarus caused many of the crowd to believe in Jesus. Others hurried to Jerusalem to report the miracle to the Sanhedrin, which held an emergency meeting under the leadership of Caiaphas, the high priest. They resolved to have Jesus killed as soon as possible, lest he become the leader of an uprising against Roman rule, thereby jeopardizing the very existence of the nation. As Caiaphas summed it up, "It is expedient for us, that one man should die for the people, and that the whole nation perish not." It was the raising of Lazarus which brought the Sanhedrin to its fateful decision.

THE RAISING OF LAZARUS
Benozzo Gozzoli (Florentine, 1420-1497); Painting on canvas; 65.5 x 80.5 cm. (25.5 x 31.4 in.);
Widener Collection 1942

THE RAISING OF LAZARUS—Benozzo Gozzoli's paintings have sometimes been described as painted tapestries. They are filled with scenic detail. The figures are often grouped frieze-like, the main personages followed by their entourage. Typically Gozzoli flattens out his landscape, extending it horizontally across his painting as well as into the spatial depth of the scene.

In The Raising of Lazarus the artist shows Jesus in the center, his right arm upraised, bidding Lazarus come forth from the tomb. Jesus holds a book, possibly symbolizing the New Law or Testament, in his other hand. This is in contrast to the book of the Old Law held by the Jewish priest in the group to the far right. Ten of Jesus' disciples stand behind him, watching, wondering, and discussing. The other two stand next to the risen Lazarus; the younger of the two tries to comfort the bewildered Lazarus.

Mary and Martha kneel in wonder and adoration. Having chided Jesus for not hurrying to their sick brother's bedside, they now acknowledge with awe that Jesus is indeed "the Resurrection and the Life."

Crowds watch from either side. Among them are religious leaders who disapprove and simple townsfolk who will spread the news of this miracle throughout Jerusalem. In the lower right are two servants, their humble station denoted by their miniscule size. The Holy City can be seen in the middle distance.

Mary Magdalene

Among the women who followed Jesus during his public ministry was one named Mary from the city of Magdala, largest and wealthiest of the ten Roman towns on the shore of Lake Galilee. This Mary is most often referred to as Mary Magdalene to distinguish her from other Marys associated with Jesus.

According to tradition, Mary Magdalene was the prostitute who burst into Jesus' presence while he was visiting the home of a Pharisee. In great spiritual distress, she washed Jesus' feet with her tears and dried them with her hair. The Pharisee upbraided Jesus for allowing so sinful a woman even to touch him, much less bathe and caress his feet. Jesus, however, pointed out that such a demonstration of love was born out of a deep-seated repentance, and that therefore her sins were fully forgiven her.

If the woman was in fact Mary Magdalene, she became a steadfast follower of Jesus. It is recorded that Jesus exorcised seven demons from her. Eventually she witnessed Jesus' crucifixion, led the women to the tomb to anoint his body, and encountered the risen Lord in a garden near the empty tomb. Her falling on her knees to clasp the risen Jesus, joyful that he was alive again, is fully in keeping with the woman who once bathed his feet in love and repentance.

THE REPENTANT MAGDA-LEN—A French painter of the seventeenth century, Georges de La Tour has been in and out of favor with art critics since his own day. In recent years his work has been appreciated anew. He is especially admired for his treatment of light. La Tour creates a mood, often a pensive and melancholy one, and subtly fills in the space of his painting with nuances of light and shadow.

In The Repentant Magdalen, La Tour draws upon the tradition that Mary Magdalene had once been a harlot. He shows her at night, sitting in a room alone, lost in thought as she stares in a mirror, her hand resting on a skull, an often-used symbol of human mortality. Through her hand she feels the reality of death. She ponders death as she looks on her own image, an image that flickers and dances in the moving light of the candle. Although the Magdalene is rapt and motionless, her thoughts are as alive as the glint in her eye and the movement of the flame.

One cannot imagine any sound interrupting this silent moment. The muted reddish-brown tones contrast with the relative brightness of the Magdalene's right forearm and shoulder. The folds of her blouse and wisps of her hair are realistic, but the overall effect is a reality absorbed into the mystical. This realistic treatment popularized the introspective pietism of the seventeenth century for lay people who could not easily grasp the complexities of contemporary mystical writers.

THE REPENTANT MAGDALEN
Georges de La Tour (French, 1593-1652); Painting on canvas; 113.0 x 92.7 cm. (44.1 x 36.2 in.);
Ailsa Mellon Bruce Fund

THE LAST WEEK

Triumphal Entry into Jerusalem

Some time after he raised Lazarus from the dead, Jesus returned to Bethany for a dinner party given in his and Lazarus' honor. So many people crowded around the house to see him that the religious leaders were extremely upset. The next day he decided to enter openly and with powerful symbolism into the holy city of Jerusalem. He sent two of his disciples to obtain a donkey. He specifically wanted a young male donkey on which no one had yet ridden. This called to mind the prophecy of Zechariah which promised Jerusalem that her king would come to her "humble and riding on a donkey."

A large crowd of followers were with him in Bethany, many from Galilee where they had tried to proclaim him king after he fed the five thousand. At that time Jesus had discouraged them and even fled from them. Now, by the power he demonstrated in calling Lazarus forth from the tomb, and by his deliberately symbolic entry into the city of David, he seemed to give new life to their hope for a king.

As they started out on the short walk from Bethany to Jerusalem, the excitement grew. People cried out in joy. A crowd surged out from the city, mingling with those from Bethany. Cheers became shouts. People began spreading their outer garments on the road in front of Jesus as he rode toward the city, a time-honored way to pay homage to the king. Then people started to cut palm branches from the trees of nearby gardens, spreading them out before Jesus along with their garments. Soon a chant welled up from the crowd: "Hosanna to the Son of David: Blessed is he that cometh in the name of the Lord; Hosanna in the highest." This chant not only expressed the joy of the crowd but identified Jesus with the long-awaited Messianic king, the Son of David who would come in the name of the Lord to establish the Kingdom of God.

Among the crowd were some of the religious leaders. Earlier they had been concerned about Jesus' growing popularity. Now they were deeply alarmed. They called out to him to quiet the crowd and to renounce these acclamations. Jesus, enjoying this triumphal moment, replied that even if the crowds kept still the very stones on the ground would shout aloud.

CHRIST'S ENTRY INTO JERUSALEM—In this delicate miniature engraving an anonymous German engraver known as the Master of St. Erasmus shows Jesus entering Jerusalem in triumph. It was done sometime around 1440-1450, and provides an example of the "undeveloped" state of engraving at that time. Nevertheless, the artist manages to convey a deep understanding of the event.

Jesus is shown riding astride the donkey, European-fashion. It is more likely that in reality he rode in the Middle Eastern fashion, sidesaddle. The donkey almost prances in the manner of a royal steed, while Jesus raises his right hand in the traditional Christian manner of bestowing a

CHRIST'S ENTRY INTO JERUSALEM
Master of St. Erasmus (German, active c. 1450-1470); Engraving; 5.8 x 3.7 cm. (2.3 x 1.4 in.);
Rosenwald Collection

blessing on the people and the city. His thumb, forefinger, and middle finger are joined as one, representing the Trinity of Father, Son, and Holy Spirit.

A townsman, representing the crowd, greets Jesus and his entourage. He throws a garment on the road before Jesus, paying homage to this royal Son of David.

The artist evinces the medieval love of animals and birds: the donkey has the most expressive and charming face in the picture.

Cleansing
of the Temple

Jesus' cleansing of the Temple by driving out the moneylenders and vendors is recorded by all four evangelists, which underscores its importance. In the Gospels of Matthew, Mark, and Luke it was the last great public act of his ministry, and marks the final breach between Jesus and the nation's religious authorities.

Jesus had been engaged in a running controversy with the authorities on the observance of the Sabbath. They insisted on rigorous adherence to traditional regulations; he taught a more human application of the spirit of the Law. When he healed on the Sabbath, they accused him of blasphemy. Since most of this confrontation took place in Galilee, which was under the rule of Herod Antipas, the religious authorities appealed to Herod to imprison Jesus as he had imprisoned John the Baptist. Before any action of this sort could take place, however, Jesus left Galilee and Herod's jurisdiction, and began his last trip through Judea to Jerusalem for the Passover.

He entered Jerusalem a week prior to Passover. Very shortly after his arrival he "cleansed" the Temple, an act which served to culminate his conflict with the religious authorities. Having first assailed their strict observance of the Sabbath tradition, he now attacked what he held to be their perversion of the Temple sacrificial system, which had been transformed into a vast commercial operation. By insisting upon the use of "Temple money" as the sole coin of exchange in the Temple, they profited from an artificially high rate of exchange when pilgrims from all over the world changed their currencies. Also, by creating an exclusive franchise on the Temple grounds for the sale of sacrificial animals, they could set their own prices.

These travesties so offended Jesus that he made a whip of cord and flailed about him, turning over the tables of the moneychangers and disrupting the sale of animals. Because this was the week before Passover and the peak period of sacrificial activity, the Temple court was jammed with animals, moneychangers, and pilgrims. Thus, Jesus chose the busiest and most profitable season to assert dramatically that the Temple was intended to be a "house of prayer" and not a "den of thieves." From this time, the religious authorities were determined to have him killed.

CHRIST CLEANSING THE TEMPLE
El Greco (Spanish, 1541-1614); Painting on wood; 65.4 x 83.2 cm. (25.5 x 32.4 in.);
Samuel H. Kress Collection 1957

CHRIST CLEANSING THE TEMPLE—One of the outstanding artists of the late sixteenth and early seventeenth centuries was Domenikos Theotokopoulos. Born on the island of Crete, he gained his initial artistic experience in Venice and Rome. However, most of his life as an artist was spent in Spain, where he came to be known as "El Greco," the Greek.

His early work, including Christ Cleansing the Temple, clearly reflected his Italian years. It was only later in his career that El Greco developed the austere, elongated figures for which he is known today. In Christ Cleansing the Temple, he shows writhing bodies straining to escape the sting of Jesus' whip. Based on classical models so dearly loved by the Italians, these semi-nude adults and unclad children become symbols of moral decadence. The Temple here is clearly patterned after an Italian Renaissance villa. Nude or semi-nude statuary adorns its precincts, which would have been anathema to Judaism.

Everyone and everything is in disarray as a justly angry Jesus flails away, zealous to purge his Father's house of crass commercialism. All react in direct fear of him or in consideration of the effect of his actions on their business. Cages of turtledoves are upset and broken. Freed birds perch overhead and walk away. The rabbits are incongruous, since only turtledoves and spotless lambs were acceptable sacrifices in the Temple.

In this painting El Greco also shows the dominant cloud formations characteristic of Venice. Near the cage of doves you can see his signature in Greek, with his nickname "Greco" as the second line.

83

THE LAST SUPPER
Jean Penicaud I (French, early XVI Century); Limoges enamel; 29.7 x 25.1 cm. (11.6 x 9.8 in.); Widener Collection 1942

The
Last
Supper

THE LAST SUPPER—Limoges, France, was the center of the finest enamelware in Europe after about 1475. Early Limoges pieces often reached the level of high art, original in form and interpretation. The first known Limoges master was Nardon Penicaud, and many of his descendants in the Penicaud family carried on in his tradition. Jean Penicaud I (so called since there were several enamelists named Jean Penicaud—each one is designated by a different number) was an early follower of the great master.

Fifteenth and sixteenth century Limoges enamels generally have religious themes, usually inspired by well-known paintings or prints. Jean Penicaud I used such a model for this enamel, which he made in the early years of the sixteenth century.

He shows Jesus with his disciples. Two servants in the far left corner discuss what they see. John, the beloved disciple, sits close to Jesus. The Bible tells us that the beloved disciple was "leaning on Jesus' bosom." Jesus has just announced, "One of you will betray me," and all except John and one other show extreme agitation. The other disciple unmoved by Jesus' words is Judas, directly across from him.

The attention to detail in this enamel is truly astouding. There are intricate designs in the tiles on the floor, and scrolls and floral ornaments in the architecture. Penicaud gives a sense of depth in the scene through his use of perspective and in the sculptural recession of the apselike architectural setting.

Jesus made secret arrangements to celebrate the Passover meal with his disciples in the room of a private home in Jerusalem. Not wanting to be interrupted by the crowds which accompanied his every step during the daytime, he sent Peter and John ahead from Bethany into the city to set the room in order. Quietly and unnoticed in the dusk, Jesus and his other disciples then found their way to the room.

The table was low, and the company sat around it on cushions as they met to reenact the wondrous deliverance of the children of Israel from Egyptian bondage centuries earlier. At the height of the meal Jesus added to the symbolic elements of the Passover meal by taking bread, probably the unleavened loaf traditionally used for this meal, and told his disciples to eat it as his own body. He was giving his body for them, he said, and they were to eat this bread as a way to remember him. Then he took a cup of wine and told them to drink it as his own blood, for he was about to shed his blood for the forgiveness of sins. He called it "the cup of the new testament" (or "new covenant"), indicating that he was consciously establishing a new manner of relating to God which for his followers superseded the "old covenant."

His disciples were excitedly picturing themselves leaders in this new kingdom. They began quarreling about which one would be the greatest, since they thought they would soon displace the current political and religious leaders of the nation. Jesus rebuked them saying that the chief among them was to be the servant of all, since his kingdom was not at all like the kingdoms of the world.

One of the twelve, Judas Iscariot, had long been dissatisfied with the way things were turning out. Judas knew how desperately the religious leaders wanted to get rid of Jesus because of his popularity, but this very popularity was depriving them of any opportunity to do so. So Judas had gone to them and made a proposal; he would let them know when it would be safe to seize Jesus. Jesus was aware of Judas' treachery. In the midst of this symbolic meal he told Judas to leave the gathering and go do what was in his heart. The others thought that Jesus had merely sent him out on an errand.

THE LAST SUPPER—Callot shows the Last Supper taking place in a great hall, like those we see in Venetian paintings of the same period. The hall is filled with spectators who crowd the area in the doorway behind Jesus and sit in the windows. Some are servants, who pass up containers of food and drink from their master's table. Other servants bring more food from the kitchen to the left, while still others serve from a fully laden sideboard on the right. Typical also of Callot's time, small dogs hover near the table, ready to pounce on any scrap of food which might fall near them.

The twelve disciples sit around the table with Jesus. Judas is in the right center foreground, holding the treasurer's bag in his left hand and a knife in his right. John, the beloved disciple, leans against Jesus' bosom as Jesus rests his arm over John's shoulders. Large candles on the table illumine the meal; these are similar to the traditional candles used on the altar during eucharistic services by many Christian churches.

Is this the moment Jesus pointed out that one of those present would betray him? The apostles may well be asking themselves, "Is it I?"

THE LAST SUPPER
Jacques Callot (French, 1592-1635); Etching and engraving; 11.3 x 21.6 cm. (4.4 x 8.4 in.);
Rudolph L. Baumfeld Collection

Christe tuis en pascis oues hic carnibus, ipse
et Cibus, et Pastor, moxque futurus Ouis

THE LAST SUPPER—The English poet, painter and engraver William Blake lived from 1757 to 1827. He also worked as a printer, and applied what he learned of inks and presses to create his own style of illuminated printing. Flashes of light fill his work. He drew particular inspiration from the Bible and Milton, creating many works from these sources. Although he was more or less ignored during his lifetime, he is now considered to be the greatest of English poet-painters. His work is always intensely personal, reflecting his mystical, at times almost ethereal, vision of Christianity.

In this painting Blake shows Jesus and his twelve disciples at an opulent Oriental feast. Jesus seems transcendent, gleaming with light, wholly otherworldly. As he shares his heavenly vision with his followers, he seems already transformed. His light illumines the disciples gathered around him. Only Judas turns away from the light, unable to stand its burning purity. Lost in the darkness of his own thoughts and schemes, Judas counts the money in his bag, for he is the treasurer of the tiny group. Soon he will earn thirty silver pieces more for his act of treachery.

John, the beloved disciple, sits close to Jesus. Blake shows him to be the most sensitive and poetic of the disciples, almost feminine in his feeling and devotion. Some disciples strain to hear each word; some bow in wondering adoration; some gaze far away in thought; and some discuss the meaning of what they hear.

THE LAST SUPPER
William Blake (British, 1757-1827);
Painting on canvas;
30.5 x 48.2 cm. (11.9 x 18.8 in.);
Rosenwald Collection 1954

THE SACRAMENT OF THE LAST SUPPER—Salvador Dali is the most famous of the contemporary surrealist painters. He combines meticulous attention to realistic detail together with fantasy, often evoking hallucinatory effects through the use of double images. By juxtaposing realistic but unexpected images, Dali conjures up what has been called a "dream photograph."

The Sacrament of the Last Supper is perhaps the most popular painting in the National Gallery of Art collection. The Gallery has placed it behind the main information desk, where it may be easily seen by the visiting public. In the painting Dali shows the twelve apostles, dressed in stylized, monklike garb, kneeling around a table. The twelve are placed symmetrically, almost as though the two groups of six were mirror images of each other. In the center is Jesus, symbolized by the wine and bread set before him. These are placed on the table so as to emphasize the perspective system of folds in the cloth, all pointing to Jesus' transparent body.

In the background Dali shows a body of water surrounded by barren hills. A haze transforms itself into an aura of light and suffuses the center of the painting, seeming to come from Jesus and at the same time to shine through him: boats appear through his left arm and torso. Even as he institutes the sacrament using ordinary bread and table wine, Jesus' body begins to be transformed.

Dali's painting captures visually the devotional experience of interpenetrating levels of symbolism in the Last Supper. It suggests that liturgy is as much a matter of religious imagination as of verbal formulas and ritual actions.

THE SACRAMENT OF THE LAST SUPPER
Salvador Dali (Spanish, 1904-   );
Painting on canvas;
166.7 x 267.0 cm. (65.0 x 104.1 in.);
Chester Dale Collection 1962

Humilis en Christus: quia aquâ lavat ipse ministros,
Nos autem proprio sangvine mundificat.

CHRIST WASHING THE APOSTLES' FEET
Jacques Callot (French, 1592-1635); Etching and engraving; 11.1 x 21.5 cm. (4.3 x 8.4 in.); Rudolph L. Baumfeld Collection

CHRIST WASHING THE APOSTLES' FEET—This etching contrasts the pomp of human pretension with the simplicity of Jesus' gentle service. The architecture is an overpowering statement of grandeur, with classical pilasters supporting the arches of buildings which dwarf mere human beings. The Latin inscription also stresses the contrast between this imperial setting and Jesus' human frailty. It says: "Christ is humble, for he washes his disciples with water; us, however, he purifies with his own blood."

In this imposing setting the apostles bear themselves like men of worldly power, their gestures grandiloquent, their heads tilted at haughty angles. In contrast, servants hasten with towels and jars of water for the Master, and Jesus himself kneels before Peter tenderly washing his feet. Jesus alone seems graceful in spirit as well as body. For him, service is grace.

A clown gazing from the window at the far left may be meant to suggest the folly of human ambition—in the apostles who still do not understand the nature of the kingdom Jesus is giving them. As we know from Shakespeare, in the sixteenth century clowns were thought to be able to see through human folly.

By his delicate use of cross-hatched straight lines Callot demonstrates remarkable ability to vary light and shadow. The shadow cast by the disciple on the left has more than one degree of intensity. The halo radiating from Jesus' head is almost blinding in its absence of any central line whatsoever.

Washing of the Feet

During the evening of the Last Supper in the upper room before Judas Iscariot left on his mission of betrayal, Jesus took off his outer robe and wrapped a towel around his waist. Dressed in this way, like a slave, he poured water in a basin and began to wash the feet of the disciples.

This strange act was not the usual courteous footwashing given to a guest who came into a house from the hot, dusty road. It was rather a parable acted out by Jesus to demonstrate to his disciples how life was to be lived in the kingdom he was establishing. Some of the disciples had been arguing among themselves over which one of them would be the greatest in the kingdom. Jesus here gives them their answer: the Master himself was performing a humble act of service and refreshment for each of his followers.

When it was Peter's turn to have his feet washed, he protested. One day he would understand the meaning of the act, Jesus told him, but still he refused. Sternly, Jesus told Peter that if he would not allow his feet to be washed, he could have no further relationship with the Master. Not only had Peter refused to accept Jesus' self-abasing service, but he had rebelled against Jesus' authority. It is little wonder that Jesus made such an issue of Peter's response.

Peter's resistance immediately vanished, and he pleaded with Jesus to wash not only his feet, but his hands and head as well. Jesus made it clear, however, that the feet were enough, for what was really important was the act of service and not the literal washing of any part of the body.

Jesus then instructed the disciples at length about the nature of the kingdom he was establishing. He told them he would be with them always and taught them about the nature of prayer. When he indicated he would be leaving them soon, Peter asked where he was going. Jesus said he could not follow him at the moment. Peter said he would go anywhere for Jesus, even to his death. Jesus quietly told him that he would deny even knowing Jesus before the morning cock crowed. Then, Jesus and his disciples sang a hymn and set out in the dark for an olive grove on a mountain across the Kidron Valley.

THE WASHING OF FEET
Anonymous (Swabian, c. 1480-1490); Woodcut; 7.3 x 5.3 cm. (2.8 x 2.1 in.);
Rosenwald Collection

THE WASHING OF FEET— This is a charming woodcut from Swabia by an unknown artist. It shows eleven apostles clustered tightly around Jesus as he washes the feet of the twelfth. So tightly packed has the artist made the eleven that some of them strain to peer over the heads of their companions to catch a glimpse of what is happening. Only one apostle does not have a halo. Medieval artists used this device to point out Judas Iscariot, the betrayer.

Jesus uses a cloth tied about his waist, apronlike, as a towel, and has rolled up his sleeves for work. Peter, the disciple whose feet are being washed, has lifted his long garment to his knees as he discusses with Jesus the meaning of this symbolic action. The others look on, listening and awaiting their turn.

Agony in the Garden

Jesus and his eleven disciples walked down the steep slopes of the Kidron ravine and began their ascent of the Mount of Olives. Part-way up they stopped at a favorite place of quiet retreat, an olive grove known as the Garden of Gethsemane. Jesus asked eight of the disciples to stay near the entrance to the garden; he took Peter, James, and John, the same three who were with him on the Mount of Transfiguration, into the garden with him.

He asked the three to keep watch and to pray as he went further into the garden to be alone. His heart was near breaking with heaviness and sorrow, he told them. Indeed, in the agony of his prayer as he struggled alone, he broke out in a heavy sweat to the point of sweating drops of blood. His body shared the turmoil of his spirit as he prayed, "O my Father, if it be possible, let this cup pass from me: nevertheless, not as I will, but as thou wilt."

After a period of prayer, Jesus returned to find the three sleeping soundly. These men who had spent so many sleepless nights fishing on wind-whipped Lake Galilee could not stay awake even part of the night to keep vigil with their Lord. He woke them and rebuked them, asking them to stay awake while he returned to his prayer. In solitude Jesus again committed himself to obey the will of his Father. Returning, he again found the three asleep. He went away a third time to pray, and when he came back they still slept. So he told them to sleep on, knowing full well the decisive moment for action had overtaken them.

THE AGONY IN THE GARDEN

THE AGONY IN THE GARDEN—Benedetto Montagna was a sixteenth century engraver from the northern Italian city of Vicenza. His forty-one prints that still survive show that he was a competent draftsman with considerable technical ability.

The artist shows Jesus in prayer while Peter (who holds the keys in his hand), James, and John sleep in the foreground. The stone in front of Jesus serves as an altar upon which rests a chalice surmounted by a host, or communion wafer. The host and chalice are symbols of Jesus' body and blood, and here remind the viewer that what Jesus offered mentally in the garden he would give up physically the next day on the cross. They also allude to the Eucharist, or Communion rite, in which Jesus' death is remembered, and recall his words in the garden when he prayed, "Let this cup pass from me."

An angel holds up the cross, presenting to Jesus the shape of his death while offering him the solace of heavenly comfort. Jerusalem, the place of his trial later this night, is on the hill across the Kidron Valley, and even now the soldiers are on the road to Gethsemane to arrest him.

THE AGONY IN THE GARDEN—Benvenuto di Giovanni was a Sienese painter and illuminator active at the end of the fifteenth and beginning of the sixteenth centuries. In this painting he shows the eleven disciples asleep while Jesus engages in his intense struggle. Eight sleep by the entrance to the garden. Peter, James, and John have come further into the garden with Jesus, but they too sleep, unable to watch and pray with him. John, the young beloved disciple, is on the right, his eyes fast closed in sleep. James, in the center, seems to be caught at the moment of half-wakefulness before dropping off again: unlike John or Peter, his body is tense and restless. Peter, on the left, slumbers on with the peaceful sleep of a sailor who can doze in the midst of a storm.

Jesus prays in agony of spirit as an angel holds out the cup of suffering. At first he asks that it may be taken away, but then, in perfect submission to his Father's will, he accepts it. The drops of blood which Jesus sweats are seen on the ground in front of him.

THE AGONY IN THE GARDEN
Benvenuto di Giovanni (Sienese, 1436-c. 1518); Painting on wood; 43.2 x 48.3 cm. (16.8 x 18.8 in.);
Samuel H. Kress Collection 1939

Betrayal and Arrest

For Jesus the victory had been won in the quiet agony of solitary prayer. He now actively embraced the will of God wherever it might take him, allowing himself to be borne forward from crisis to crisis. With monumental dignity he neither shrank back nor displayed weakness. A few hours after his garden agony he gave up his spirit on the cross.

As Jesus told his disciples to sleep on, he saw many lights bobbing and flickering down the Kidron valley, working their way up toward the garden: a large band of men. They were led into the garden by one who had been there often before with Jesus, one who knew he would be there again after the Passover meal. Judas Iscariot had kept his bargain with the religious leaders. He had led them to Jesus at a time when the people could not rise up to protect him.

In the dark shadows of the olive grove it would be easy to seize the wrong person. It would also be possible for Jesus to slip away into the night. So the arrest had been carefully planned. Judas went directly to Jesus, held him by both arms in Eastern fashion, and kissed him on the cheek. This was his prearranged means of identifying Jesus in the dark. It would also guarantee that Jesus was held fast until the Temple guards seized him. When Judas kissed Jesus, Jesus looked deep into his soul and asked with words which would hound him to early suicide: "Judas, betrayest thou the Son of man with a kiss?"

The religious leaders who were present ordered the guards to arrest Jesus. Peter drew a short sword he carried hidden in his garment and slashed out to protect his Master. His aim was off, for he was a better fisherman than a warrior, and he only managed to cut off the right ear of the high priest's personal servant. Jesus told Peter to put up his sword, and then reached down, picked up the ear from the ground, and put it back on the man's head, healing him at once. For a moment all movement ceased in wonder. Then the guards surged forward again and bound Jesus, while the disciples fled into the darkness.

THE BETRAYAL OF CHRIST
Valerio Belli (Italian, c. 1468-1546);
Bronze relief; 6.1 x 9.9 cm. (2.4 x 3.9 in.);
Samuel H. Kress Collection

THE BETRAYAL OF CHRIST—Valerio Belli was an Italian gem carver who worked during the sixteenth century. He was born in the city of Vicenza, and his name and birthplace are embossed on this medal—"Valerius Vicentinus." Belli's carving of exquisite works of art in rock crystal brought him international renown and was in such demand that the artist often made molds of his carved gems and then cast them in bronze. Such is the case with this medal.

Belli has depicted the moment immediately after Judas Iscariot kissed Jesus. Judas holds Jesus around the waist, securing him for capture. A guard seizes Jesus from behind, while another is about to cast a loop of rope over his head. Jesus will soon be trussed up and led hurriedly away into the night.

Jesus holds Judas' head in both his hands and peers into his eyes. For three years they have been close friends. Judas has borne the daily responsibility of caring for the physical needs of the band of disciples, and none of his companions suspected him of harboring treacherous thoughts. Now in the eye of the storm Jesus and Judas look closely at each other, and Jesus asks, "Betrayest thou me with a kiss?"

Behind Judas, Peter has drawn his knife and is about to attack the high priest's servant, who has fallen to the ground.

THE BETRAYAL AND CAPTURE OF CHRIST
Martin Schongauer (German, c. 1450-1491); Engraving; 16.3 x 11.5 cm. (6.4 x 4.5 in.);
Rosenwald Collection

THE BETRAYAL AND CAPTURE OF CHRIST—During the fifteenth century the art of engraving developed into a mature art form and became widely respected. This development coincided with the invention of the printing press and movable type, so that engraving captured the imagination of the enthusiastic, affluent, and rapidly expanding book-reading public. Martin Schongauer, a widely admired German engraver, founded an influential school of engraving in his home city of Augsburg.

In this dramatic engraving Schongauer illustrates the moment after Peter had sliced off the ear of Malchus, the personal servant of Caiaphas the high priest. Peter still holds his short sword at the ready as he prepares to thrust it into the fallen Malchus, who, in partial shock, raises his cudgel to fend off Peter's attack. Although the Scriptures speak of Malchus' right ear being severed, Schongauer uses artist's license in arranging his composition, showing Malchus with the left ear missing.

Jesus, bound and trussed, shoved and pulled, stops to perform his healing miracle on the injured man. He is a powerful presence of inner calm in the very center of a violent storm. The guards shout obscenities at him, their faces ugly with hate. Schongauer shows one, and possibly two, of the guards as Blacks, perhaps suggesting a small contingent of Ethiopian Jews among the Temple guard (the Ethiopian Jewish community traces its origins to the visit of the Queen of Sheba to King Solomon).

Judas Iscariot, clutching his bag with thirty pieces of silver, hurries off to the left. The hornlike "tail" of the guard's hat combined with Judas' goatlike beard, recall the medieval portrayal of Satan in the guise of a male goat. Night is indicated by the raised torch and the fallen lantern.

Annas was appointed high priest in A.D. 6 and was deposed by the Roman authorities in A.D. 15. However, the Jews did not recognize the deposition, so Annas continued to be regarded with all the respect and deference due the high priest. Five of his sons and Caiaphas, his son-in-law, all became high priests at one time or another, and it was Caiaphas who held the office at the time of Jesus' arrest. Although Caiaphas had been officially appointed by Rome, he in fact shared the role of high priest with his father-in-law. Thus, the Temple guards first took Jesus to Annas' house for a preliminary hearing; Annas in turn sent them to Caiaphas' house, where the Sanhedrin was waiting to hold a formal hearing.

While Jesus was being rushed from Gethsemane to Annas to Caiaphas, Peter followed, dashing from shadow to shadow. A fire burned in the high priest's courtyard, giving heat and light to the guards who waited outside for the result of the

Peter's Denial

hearing. Peter was admitted into the courtyard through the influence of one of Jesus' disciples who knew the high priest. As a young maid opened the door for Peter, she asked him whether he was a disciple of Jesus. He denied it. Then, while he warmed himself by the fire, he was again asked the question, and again he denied it. Then one man, a relative of Malchus, whose ear Peter had cut off only an hour or so earlier, looked closely at Peter and asked, "Did not I see thee in the garden with him . . . ?" Stung by the question and with every eye upon him, Peter for the third time denied knowing Jesus, emphasizing his denial with oaths and cursing.

At that moment Jesus was being led from one part of Caiaphas' house to another. He turned and looked at Peter, and the morning cock crowed. Peter remembered that Jesus had said to him, "Before the cock crows, thou shalt deny me thrice." Peter fled from the courtyard, weeping bitterly.

DENIAL OF PETER
Anonymous (Swabian, c. 1455-1465);
Woodcut;
7.8 x 5.8 cm. (3.0 x 2.3 in.);
Rosenwald Collection

DENIAL OF PETER—In a charming, if somewhat crude, woodcut from fifteenth century Swabia, an anonymous artist depicts the moment when Peter for the third time denied any knowledge of Jesus. Peter stands on the left, raising his left hand in firm denial while clutching his robes around his body with his right hand. The night is cold. In the lower right one of the high priest's servants warms his hands by the open fire. This servant appears to be smirking as he watches Peter's denial.

Through the window we see a guard accompanying Jesus. At the moment of denial, Jesus turns and looks upon Peter. Up in the top left the cock crows its welcome to the morning light.

CHRIST BEFORE ANNAS
Martin Schongauer (German, c. 1450-1491); Engraving; 16.1 x 11.4 cm. (6.3 x 4.5 in.);
Gift of W. G. Russell Allen

Annas, the father-in-law of Caiaphas the high priest, had once been high priest himself and five of his own sons had become high priests.

During the three years of Jesus' rising popular appeal and growing confrontation with the nation's religious leaders, Annas became convinced that Jesus had to be killed. Caiaphas agreed. "It is expedient that one man should die for the people," he stated. It was well within the nature of the relationship between these two men that Annas can be considered father to Caiaphas' thought.

In respect for the old man's position and power, the Temple guard took Jesus to Annas' house first for an informal interrogation before sending him on to the formal sitting of the Sanhedrin at the home of Caiaphas. At this preliminary hearing Annas probably heard the many irresponsible accusations hurled at Jesus, and he had the political shrewdness to know which ones might be effective in convicting him. Jesus' apparent blasphemy against the Temple of the Living God of the Jews was isolated as the main charge which could trip him into an open declaration of his Messiahship. This, in turn, would set him up for the charge of treason against the Roman Emperor, because he would be claiming rival political rights as a sovereign ruler of the Jewish nation. No doubt Annas guided his son-in-law in preparing the formal statement of charges under which Jesus was eventually to be condemned to death.

CHRIST BEFORE ANNAS—Here Schongauer depicts Annas as an autocrat, corrupted by years of successful exercise of power. He sits in haughty dignity on his chair, which is modeled after a bishop's cathedra or throne, with his legs crossed in the manner of one used to making his own space. Both his eyes and his finger search for a point of weakness, while Jesus stands silent, eyes downcast, like a lamb led before his slaughterers.

Schongauer shows the same guards surrounding Jesus who captured him in the garden (see The Betrayal and Capture of Christ, page 95). The torch is now nearly burned up and is cast on the floor (it took only fifteen to twenty minutes to rush Jesus from the Garden of Gethsemane to Annas' presence). Malchus carries the lamp he had dropped when Peter attacked him. One of the soldiers still tugs at Jesus' hair, not only to abuse him but also to humiliate him.

Annas' dog, used to scenes of passion and turmoil, lies indifferently near his master's throne. He ignores the clamor of the guards. Annas quietly tries to penetrate to matters of substance which can be used to rid himself and his people of this nuisance.

Before Herod Antipas

In his will Herod the Great divided his realm, with Rome's agreement, among several of his sons. He gave Perea and Galilee to a son also named Herod, sometimes called Antipas to distinguish him from his father, and Herod Antipas had the title of tetrarch. Jesus grew up and conducted most of his public ministry in Galilee as a subject of Herod Antipas.

This is the same Herod who, at the urging of his wife, arrested John the Baptist and kept him prisoner for about a year before having him executed. Herod was intensely curious about Jewish religious developments and personalities, and therefore talked often with the Baptist during that year. Jesus' healings and miracles were reported to him by the religious leaders, who hoped Herod would then take Jesus into custody. Herod sought an interview with Jesus; but when he heard of it, Jesus traveled quickly south to Judea out of Herod's jurisdiction. He referred to Herod as "that fox," alluding to his reputation for deceit.

After Jesus' trial before the Sanhedrin in Caiaphas' house, the religious authorities had him taken to Pilate, the Roman governor, for sentencing. However, Pilate did not acquiesce at once to their wishes, but questioned Jesus himself. When he discovered that Jesus was from Galilee, Pilate sought to turn the occasion to political advantage. He knew that Herod was visiting Jerusalem for the Passover, so he sent Jesus to him for examination since Jesus was a subject of Herod's.

Herod was greatly pleased, for he had long wanted to meet Jesus, hoping to see him perform a miracle. Herod spoke at great length with Jesus, urging him to "perform" while offering the lure of his personal protection. Jesus had resisted such a temptation in the wilderness years before, and did so again now. He said not one word throughout Herod's cajoling, even though during the entire interview the religious authorities "vehemently accused" him of crimes deserving death.

Herod's patience finally came to an end. He ordered his troops to beat Jesus, to mock him, to dress him up in a gorgeous robe (this partly to belittle the religious leaders), and to send him back to Pilate for judgment. From Herod's point of view, the only positive outcome of the long night was the improvement of what had been a strained relationship with Pilate.

CHRIST BEFORE HEROD
Lucas Cranach the Elder (German, 1472-1553); Woodcut; 24.7 x 17.0 cm. (9.6 x 6.6 in.);
Rosenwald Collection

CHRIST BEFORE HEROD—One of the most successful painters and print makers of his day, Cranach was born in the northern Franconian town of Kronach in the late fifteenth century. He learned the art of woodcut and engraving from his father, and worked for a period in Vienna. By the time he was thirty-two Cranach was appointed court painter to Frederick the Wise, Elector of Saxony. Frederick was also the patron of Martin Luther, his official court preacher at Wittenberg. Cranach and Luther became close friends, and in later years Cranach illustrated, published, and sold many of Luther's writings, including his translation of the New Testament.

Cranach shows Herod questioning the silent Jesus.

Jesus stands bound, submissive, gazing off into space as he avoids direct contact with the tetrarch. The guards crowd in on him; their faces show their readiness to beat this Galilean peasant who so insolently ignores their ruler. One of them stares in violent hatred as he makes a universal sign of contempt with his finger in his mouth.

The dissolute Herod sits on an elaborate throne adorned with cupids, perhaps meant to symbolize his lustfulness. He had married his brother's wife and then lusted after her daughter, his brother's child. This amoral dilettante in matters of religious interest languidly hopes to be amused by a famous prisoner. When Jesus does not pander to his whims, Herod tires of the game and sends Jesus back to Pilate and his fate.

101

The Scourging of Jesus

After the Sanhedrin found Jesus guilty of blasphemy because he claimed to be the Messiah, they sent him to Pilate for judgment. Although blasphemy was a capital crime according to Jewish tradition, the Roman government had reserved the sentencing of capital punishment to itself. Pilate had sought to rid himself of the case by sending Jesus to Herod Antipas but, as we saw, Jesus refused to humor Herod, who returned him to Pilate.

It was now early morning. Since the charge of blasphemy was irrelevant in Roman jurisprudence, some charge had to be quickly propounded which the Romans would take seriously. Therefore the religious leaders accused Jesus of political ambition, insinuating that he wanted to "liberate" Palestine from Roman rule and set up a theocratic, independent nation with himself as "God's anointed" (Messianic) ruler. This was indeed a crime Rome took seriously, so Pilate carefully interrogated Jesus in

THE FLAGELLATION OF CHRIST
Umbrian School (early XVI Century);
Painting on wood; 55.9 x 48.1 cm. (21.8 x 18.8 in.);
Samuel H. Kress Collection 1952

THE FLAGELLATION OF CHRIST—During the fifteenth and sixteenth centuries various schools of painting flourished throughout Italy, each developing dominant characteristics. Sometimes an individual master rose above the level of his contemporaries, becoming famous in his own right. His influence would modify the painting of his time, subtly changing the characteristics of the school until a new master's influence would replace his. The paintings of the early sixteenth century Umbrian school reflected the influences of Pietro Perugino and of his more famous pupil, Raphael.

The strong architectural framework of the painting is typical of Umbrian art of the time. The rounded arches are Roman. The column to which Jesus is tied is a copy of a classical original. Umbrian painting opened space to show the possibility of infinity; the landscape recedes behind Jesus' head into a timeless tranquility.

The emotional tenor of Umbrian art also tends toward meditative calm. In this painting the figures are poised like dancers. The painting takes its mood from the resigned spiritual sorrow of Jesus rather than from the reality of physical agony of a Roman scourging. Even the light cord which binds Jesus does not cut his flesh, but rather is secured with a fragile bow. The only strong emotion shown is in the face of the soldiers on the left. The viewer is expected to contemplate in peace the meaning of the flagellation rather than experience its horror.

private. He became convinced that Jesus was no political aspirant, no threat to the Emperor's realm, and publicly announced he was prepared to release him.

Meanwhile, the religious leaders whipped up a mob they had brought along with them into screaming for Jesus' death. They began chanting "Crucify him, crucify him, crucify him!" In order to satisfy their bloodlust, Pilate calculated that if he had Jesus beaten and mocked, the crowd would be pacified. He ordered his tough soldiers, the elite Praetorian Guard, to scourge Jesus.

The Roman scourge was a short whip with many two-to-three foot thongs fastened to a single handle. Bits of sharp bone or slivers of metal were tied at various places along the thongs. Wielded by a powerful, relentless legionnaire, a scourge could flay the skin off a man's back within twenty lashes. It was with this instrument that Pilate's soldiers scourged Jesus.

FLAGELLATION OF CHRIST WITH THE PAVEMENT—Andrea Mantegna was a prolific and influential Italian painter of the last half of the fifteenth century who also developed engraving to a fine art. His work was sought throughout Italy by clerical and secular patrons, and many contemporary and younger artists worked in his style. This engraving is from his school, and it contains the essential spirit of the master.

Early in his career Mantegna discovered the architecture and statuary of classical Rome. The Roman officer on the far right is modeled on an ancient Roman prototype, probably from a sarcophagus. He is the embodiment of classical beauty, proportion, and strength. His young assistant turns toward him, ready to serve his every wish. The officer watches three of his soldiers scourging Jesus. They are young and vigorous, and throw themselves into their task with energy. An older officer sits and watches, while other soldiers look on in the background.

At the center of the composition is Jesus. The tortured outlines of his body focus attention on him and what he is undergoing. Pilate had said, "I find no fault in him," and then ordered him subjected to this harsh treatment. For the Roman soldiers scourging was an everyday occurrence; for Jesus it was an echo of a biblical prediction that he could expect to be "despised and rejected of men."

FLAGELLATION OF CHRIST WITH THE PAVEMENT
School of Andrea Mantegna (Paduan, 1431-1506);
Engraving; 34.1 x 28.8 cm. (13.3 x 11.2 in.);
Rosenwald Collection

Crowning with Thorns

When the scourging was completed, Jesus' body was seriously weakened, but not enough to kill or disable him. The soldiers sat him on a mock throne in the center of their parade area, and then braided a circular wreath or crown from the branches of a thornbush. It is not known exactly which plant they used, but there are a number of local bushes with sharp, thick spines, and it is unlikely that they had to search far.

The soldiers were well aware that Jesus' enemies alleged he was "the king of the Jews" and that he himself acknowledged a kingship "not of this world." The only kind of kings that Roman legionnaires knew anything about were very much "of this world." They themselves served the mightiest king alive, the Roman Emperor, and had fought many campaigns to overthrow other kings. To them Jesus' claim to some sort of spiritual kingship was a joke. He deserved to be made fun of, so they called the ring of thorns a crown, a royal diadem, and placed it on his head in derision. None too gentle in their mockery, they probably forced it down, causing blood to streak down and cake on his haggard face.

Next they put a purple robe around Jesus' shoulders and set a staff to serve as a royal scepter in his hands. They called out "Hail, King of the Jews!" as they spit upon him and slapped him with their hands.

How this mocking of Jesus must have both gratified and infuriated his enemies! They were satisfied that Jesus was being severely hurt physically and that events might now be in motion which would lead to his execution. Yet Pilate and the Roman soldiers were mocking them as well as Jesus. There was a long-nursed hostility between the arrogant, often self-righteous, uncompromising religious leaders and the self-satisfied, uncompromising Roman governor. From time to time this hostility led to open violence, and would within thirty-five years erupt into a terrible war which would destroy Jerusalem and finally burn out at Masada. On this day the soldiers were acting out their contempt for the Jews who deserved, in their minds, no better king than this silent weakling whom they had just scourged.

THE CROWNING WITH THORNS—Israhel van Meckenem the Elder was a Dutch-German engraver whose works were produced during the mid-fifteenth century. In Germany at that time prints were a new and especially important art form, and Meckenem was one of the most widely admired early engravers.

In The Crowning with Thorns, Meckenem places the mocking of Jesus and the crowning with thorns in a Gothic setting. In the distant right the scene of Jesus' being struck while blindfolded is shown. By the time he is crowned with thorns, his robe has been ripped. The soldiers beat him with staffs and force the crown of thorns down on his head. One puts a mock scepter in his hand. The crown motif is repeated in the candleholder above Jesus, suggesting that he is king in a way never dreamed by those who ridicule him. The lighted candle is a common sign of supernatural presence.

From the far balconies, left and center, Jesus' opponents watch these events with great satisfaction. His humiliation means that their position will not seriously be challenged by the Roman governor. The two figures in the left foreground are Pilate, whose back is toward us, and an aide. They stand in aristocratic aloofness from the harsh reality of what is happening to Jesus. Two pet dogs play on the tile floor, suggesting the indifference of the world at large to Jesus' suffering.

As one studies the face of this Jesus, withdrawn yet at peace, contemplative, one is reminded that he was "a man of sorrows, and acquainted with grief."

THE CROWNING WITH THORNS
Israhel van Meckenem (German, c. 1445-1503); Engraving; 21.0 x 14.6 cm. (8.2 x 5.7 in.);
Rosenwald Collection

Ecce Homo

When the soldiers had finished scourging and mocking Jesus, Pilate ordered him brought before the crowd. Pilate hoped the spectacle would arouse pity in the hearts of those who looked on this battered body. He called out, "Behold the man" (*Ecce homo*), with the sense of "Look at this pathetic sight! Is it really possible to consider such a forlorn, powerless man a rival king? Come on now, let's all agree to let him go. He's had enough."

Pilate stood with military bearing, in the impressive uniform of a Roman procurator. Beside him stood the Galilean teacher, ludicrous in his mock-royal robe and

utterly exhausted from the physical, psychological, and spiritual ordeal he had undergone. When Pilate said, "Behold the man," there was a long silent moment as the mob stared at Jesus. In order to prevent any feeling of sympathy for the beaten man, one of the religious leaders in the back of the crowd began the chant "Crucify him, crucify him." One voice after another took up the chant, until all sense of compassion was forgotten.

Pilate did not want to violate his conscience by ordering the execution of an innocent man, so he said to the leaders, "Take ye him, and crucify him: for I find no fault in him." He knew this was an impossible offer, for the religious leaders had no authority to crucify or stone anyone.

The religious leaders shouted back that Jesus should die according to their law because he "made himself the Son of God." At these words Pilate was undoubtedly filled with superstitious anxiety. Was Jesus some manifestation of the divine? Roman religion was replete with stories about the gods in human form. Divine status was claimed for the Emperor, and worship of his person became an issue of political loyalty. Was Jesus too a divinity in human form?

ECCE HOMO
Israhel van Meckenem (German, c. 1445-1503);
Engraving; 21.2 x 14.7 cm. (8.3 x 5.7 in.);
Rosenwald Collection

ECCE HOMO—In this fifteenth century engraving Israhel van Meckenem pictures Pontius Pilate at the moment he presents Jesus to the religious leaders and the mob they have brought with them. Pilate points to Jesus as he says, "Behold the man." Hoping to placate the mob's bloodlust, he found instead that the religious leaders only urged the mob on to demand Jesus' execution.

In the background, Meckenem shows Pilate's wife telling Pilate of her disturbing dream in which she was warned against harming Jesus. "Have nothing to do with that just man," she pled. But under pressure from the religious leaders, Pilate ignored her plea.

The members of the crowd appear coarse, even swinish. One of the religious leaders, his hood hiding his face, whispers instructions to one of the mob about what to shout out to Pilate. Another man stands with rope and hammer ready to assist with the crucifixion. The mob is angry, mindless, bent on having its way regardless of Pilate's wishes.

Jesus has been stripped of his mock-royal robe and his scepter. He still wears the crown of thorns, and his body bears the weals from his scourging. His eyes are closed, as he stands unsteadily on the porch, faint with abuse and weariness. The mob is unmoved by the sight of his suffering, its bloodlust unsatisfied.

One of Pilate's exotic pets, a grotesque quasi-human monkey, sits tied to the porch, eating fruit. It looks at the mob with disgust, as though Meckenem is asking, "Which is really the wild beast—the monkey or the hate-filled men?"

Condemnation to Death

Having heard that Jesus claimed to be the "Son of God," Pilate sought to probe this rumor of divinity. He asked Jesus where he came from, but Jesus stood silent. Pilate then reminded Jesus that he had the power of life and death. Jesus now spoke: Pilate had no power whatsoever, he stated, except that which was given to him "from above." "Above" could be either a reference to the Emperor or to God. Jesus went on to say that Pilate's guilt was less because he was exercising power legitimately; while those who had handed him over to Pilate were unlawfully using civil power to secure an unjust sentence.

Sometime during this private interview with Jesus, Pilate received an urgent message from his wife, telling him that she had had a most disturbing dream about Jesus. She was concerned for her husband's reputation and well-being, and when she woke, she sent the message to her husband to have nothing to do with this "just man," but it was too late.

Pilate was determined to release Jesus and announced his intention to the leaders and the mob. They threatened him by saying they would report to the Emperor that Pilate befriended an enemy of the state by protecting one who made himself a rival king. The crowd shouted and shoved, demanding Jesus' death, milling about on the verge of riot. No longer able to resist the crowd's demands and fearful of the leaders' threats, Pilate succumbed to their wishes.

It was 6 A.M. when Pilate sat down on the judgment seat, called for a basin of water, and ceremonially washed his hands, thereby publicly disclaiming any responsibility for the death of Jesus. He tried to cast the guilt on those who forced him to pass the death sentence.

Even as he passed sentence on Jesus Pilate could not resist one further taunt to the crowd. He pointed to Jesus and shouted, "Behold your king!" This only enraged them the more as they screamed for Jesus' immediate execution. Pilate pressed them further by asking if he should have their king put to death. The leaders replied with words which were a denial of everything they held most dear, "We have no king but Caesar." This they did in the heat of the moment, intent on securing the death of one whom they believed was a blasphemer.

CHRIST BEFORE PILATE
Martin Schongauer (German, c. 1450-1491);
Engraving;
16.3 x 11.6 cm. (6.4 x 4.5 in.);
Rosenwald Collection

CHRIST BEFORE PILATE—Martin Schongauer illustrates the moment Pilate washes his hands, disclaiming any personal responsibility for passing the sentence of death on the innocent Jesus. His expression of ironic introspection at this moment shows that Pilate knows this act is a charade. It is indeed he who has ordered Jesus' execution, out of fear of the mob and the religious leaders' influence with the Emperor.

Pilate's guards hold Jesus securely, while members of the mob jostle. In the far left two of the religious leaders smile in self-congratulation over the success of their machinations. Two carved children perched on top of Pilate's judgment seat seem to watch the proceedings, while Pilate's dogs play at his feet in disregard of what is taking place. Of all the faces in the engraving, only the face of Jesus is relaxed and honest.

PILATVS

NVLLAM CAVSAM
MORTIS INVENIO Ī
EO CORIPIAM ERGO
ILLVM ET DIMITTAM ·W·

CHRIST BEFORE PILATE
Zoan Andrea (Italian, active c. 1490-after 1515); Engraving; 29.1 x 31.4 cm. (11.3 x 12.2 in.); Rosenwald Collection

CHRIST BEFORE PILATE—Zoan Andrea was an Italian engraver whose major works were produced at the end of the fifteenth century. He was a prolific and able craftsman, whose style was formed in the shadow of Andrea Mantegna's art. Like Mantegna he used a vigorous line to create scenes of narrative energy. A student of classical sculpture, Zoan Andrea gave his engravings a sculptural solidity and depth.

Andrea shows Pilate, imperial and arrogant, sitting on the judgment seat. One of his chief lieutenants stands behind him, watching the interrogation of Jesus. The results of his probing have led Pilate to the conclusion that Jesus is innocent of any crime deserving death. He points to the bound prisoner, and his words of acquital are chiseled in stone:

"I find no cause requiring the death penalty."

The guards discuss the surprising decision, while two religious leaders bow in mock obsequiousness to the Roman procurator. Even as they show deference to him, they point their fingers accusingly at Jesus and prepare for the next move in forcing Pilate to accede to their wishes.

Jesus stands in submission. He has long since made his peace with the events now rapidly unfolding. He finds strength deep inside himself to persevere, not struggling to find in each development some hope of rescue.

Rather than showing Jesus as beaten and bloody from his hours of harsh ordeal, Andrea pictures him as a classical figure of strength. Here Jesus is fully the equal of Pilate in regal dignity and self-possession.

109

The Way of the Cross

After Pilate passed sentence, the soldiers led Jesus away from the Praetorium to the place of his execution. They forced him to carry his own crossbar. When they arrived, this crossbar would be fixed to a vertical post already set in position.

As they walked through the narrow city streets, the religious leaders and the mob who had demanded Jesus' death pushed along with them. Curious townspeople joined them from every direction. Somewhere along this painful path Jesus stumbled and fell under the weight of the cross. When it became evident, after some hard prodding, that he no longer had the strength to continue, the soldiers pressed an onlooker into service to carry the cross the rest of the distance. This man was a Jew named Simon who had come to Jerusalem for Passover from the North African city of Cyrene.

The procession was joined by many of the women who had followed Jesus during his ministry. They wailed in anguish as they saw him jeered and beaten by crowd and soldiers alike along the way. With broken hearts they wept as they thought of the death he would soon suffer.

The way of the cross led from Pilate's palace, through the streets, to one of the gates in the wall surrounding the city. They passed through the gate to a nearby site which the Romans used as a place of crucifixion, popularly known as the Place of the Skull ("Golgotha" in Aramaic, "Calvary" in Latin, meaning "skull"). It may have been so named because of all the skulls to be found there, or because it was close to or on a hill whose shape reminded people of a skull. For whatever reason it had this grisly name, the Romans used it to reinforce their control over the people. Situated near the main city gate, Golgotha reminded all who came and went of the futility of defying Rome. Jesus and the two thieves were to join a long list of those who died hanging between heaven and earth at the Place of the Skull.

CHRIST CARRYING THE CROSS
Benvenuto di Giovanni (Sienese, 1436-c. 1518); Painting on wood;
43.2 x 48.3 cm. (16.8 x 18.8 in.); Samuel H. Kress Collection 1939

CHRIST CARRYING THE CROSS—The fifteenth century Sienese painter and illuminator Benvenuto di Giovanni painted a series of five wood panels showing the Passion of Christ. One of these depicts Jesus' carrying the cross to the place of execution.

Benvenuto situates the city of Jerusalem, looking very much like a fifteenth century city, on the far hill. Jesus is led by a rope tied around his throat. He is pulled by one coarse tormentor and pummeled from the rear by another. An elegant Roman officer watches, his right hand resting on his upright shield. Behind him throngs the common mob. Other officers and religious leaders follow the procession on horseback, while in the opposite corner of the painting are clustered Jesus' closest followers, including Mary his mother and John the beloved disciple. They lift their hands in prayer and supplication. Curious children have climbed nearby trees to see over the heads of the adults.

At the center of these conflicting emotions is Jesus, carrying his cross. He almost embraces it, suggesting his continued acceptance of his divine mission. Here, as generally in Western art, he is shown carrying the entire cross, rather than just the crossbar. Benvenuto has Jesus looking out toward the viewer, not for help or sympathy, but as if to say, "Greater love hath no man than this, that a man lay down his life for his friends." This is a devotional painting, designed to evoke a personal response.

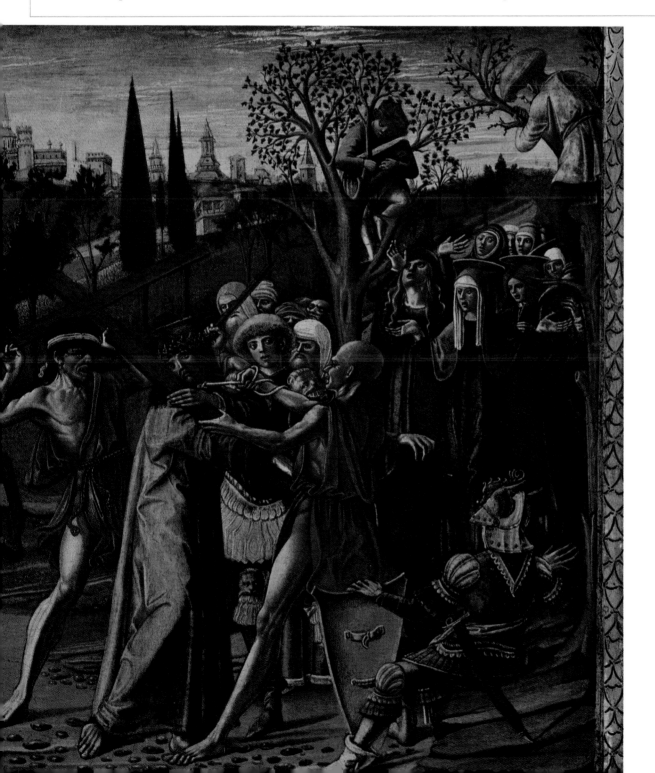

111

CHRIST BEARING THE CROSS—The gem carver and medalist Valerio Belli cast several exquisite medals of scenes from the life of Jesus. In this signed medal he shows a strong Roman soldier pulling Jesus by a rope around his neck. Jesus staggers under the weight of the cross while someone on the far left attempts to pick up some of the load. Perhaps that man is Simon of Cyrene. A Roman officer pushes Jesus forward, ready to goad him with his mace.

The small hole drilled in the medal probably at a later date allowed it to be fixed to a flat surface or worn on an article of clothing. As an object of devotion the medal would have recalled to its owner Jesus' words, "Take up thy cross, and follow me."

CHRIST BEARING THE CROSS
Valerio Belli (Italian, c. 1468-1546); Bronze relief; 8.7 x 9.6 cm. (3.4 x 3.7 in.);
Samuel H. Kress Collection

JESUS FALLS UNDER THE CROSS—Son of the famous Venetian painter Gian Battista Tiepolo, Giandomenico Tiepolo always lived under the shadow of his more widely admired father. Done during the last half of the eighteenth century, Giandomenico's work stands fully on its own as the last flowering of Venetian decorative art. The artist conveys powerful emotion through striking effects of light, space, and general atmosphere. His line is broken and restless; he is especially apt at picturing lively narrative.

During the years 1747-1749 Giandomenico painted the Fourteen Stations of the Cross in a major Venetian church. This work was so widely admired that in 1749 he prepared a series of etchings of the scenes. In the Third Station, entitled Jesus Falls Under the Cross, he shows Jesus on the Via Dolorosa (the "Way of Sorrows"), from Pilate's judgment hall to Golgotha. A band of soldiers with blaring trumpets and the imperial banner (SPQR: *Senatus Populusque Romanus* or "The Senate and the People of Rome") leads the procession out from the city through a Roman triumphal arch.

Jesus, weak from fatigue and mistreatment, has just fallen under the weight of the cross. His face shows concentration as he tries to rise to take one more step. A religious leader who helped manipulate Pilate's judgment stands impassively in front of Jesus, gloating as he falls. A prayer shawl is wrapped around this leader's shoulders, an incongruous symbol of religious orthodoxy in the midst of personal vindictiveness.

Some in the crowd reach out to help ease the burden from Jesus' back, their faces straining with effort and touched with compassion. In a moment Jesus will again take his place in the jostling, sweaty procession to Golgotha, the Place of the Skull.

JESUS FALLS UNDER THE CROSS
Giandomenico Tiepolo (Venetian, 1727-1804);
Etching; 21.3 x 18.0 cm. (8.3 x 7.0 in.); Rosenwald Collection

STAZIONE III.

CADE SOTTO LA CROCE LA PRIMA VOLTA.

De' falli nostri al troppo grave peso
Gesù non regge, e cade al suol disteso.

STAZIONE XI.

GESÙ INCHIODATO IN CROCE.

Disteso sù l' Altar, qual'innocente
Agnel, posa Gesù soavemente.

The Crucifixion

A person who was to be crucified was spared no public humiliation or physical suffering on the way to his place of execution. Jesus had to carry the heavy beam of his own cross; he was paraded through the busiest streets of the city to serve as a warning against defying Roman rule; staggering toward his death, he was scourged and goaded all the while by foul-mouthed soldiers; and in front of him, his crime was written on a board for all to see.

When the procession reached Golgotha, Jesus was crucified with two other prisoners, one on either side. The soldiers nailed his wrists to the crossbar and then hoisted him up to the top of the vertical post so that his body was fully stretched out and his feet were off the ground. Pilate had ordered his "crime" posted above his head, so the soldiers nailed up a board on which was written "Jesus of Nazareth, the King of the Jews." The text was inscribed in three languages: Latin, the official language of the ruling Romans; Greek, the common language of the Eastern Mediterranean; and Aramaic, the Semitic language spoken by the Jews of the time.

The initials "INRI" which appear on many crucifixes and in many works of art are an abbreviation of *Iesus Nazarenus Rex Iudaeorum,* the Latin words used in this sign. The religious leaders objected violently to this public declaration that Jesus was their king, but Pilate, sick of intrigue and pleased to be able to vex them, replied, "What I have written I have written," and the sign remained in place.

A squad of four soldiers under the command of a centurion (named Longinus by tradition) set about their work in a routine manner. They stripped the victim of his clothes before raising him to the cross. It was normal practice to divide any property left on the victim's person equally among the executioners. Because Jesus had only a single robe woven in one piece, they decided to gamble for it rather than destroy it by ripping it into four parts.

JESUS IS NAILED TO THE CROSS— Giandomenico Tiepolo's characteristic effects of light, space, and atmosphere are readily seen in this etching, another in the series of the Fourteen Stations of the Cross. Here Jesus is being stretched out on the vertical post. His body is already assuming the traditional pose represented in most crucifixes. He is inert, passively submitting himself to the kneeling soldier who positions him for nailing. The soldier's bag of tools lies in the foreground. A second soldier holds Jesus' feet in place.

One of the religious leaders, perhaps Caiaphas the high priest, stands by the ladder in full assurance that the right thing is being done. There is no question in his mind that it is expedient that this man die. In the distance the mob mocks Jesus, jeering and belittling him, crying out for the crucifixion to proceed. Above the place of execution clouds swirl, causing an untimely darkness that will last for the three hours that Jesus hangs on the cross.

JESUS IS NAILED TO THE CROSS
Giandomenico Tiepolo (Venetian, 1727-1804); Etching; 22.4 x 17.3 cm. (8.7 x 6.7 in.);
Rosenwald Collection

THE RAISING OF THE CROSS—A seventeenth century Italian artist, Luca Giordano painted some of his most widely admired frescoes in Spain under the patronage of Charles II and Philip V, the powerful Catholic Hapsburg rulers.

In this drawing Giordano depicts the raising of the cross. His composition is derived from a famous version of the scene by the Venetian Tintoretto, which also inspired Peter Paul Rubens, another artist of the Catholic Baroque. The strong diagonal recession into depth makes Jesus the primary focus, as his cross is raised with great effort. Some soldiers secure the foot of the post in the hole in the ground; others strain to push the cross upright or to pull it up with a rope; still others balance precariously on a hand-held ladder, trying to steady the cross. An officer on horseback shouts his orders to his squad. In the distance another squad under the direction of its officers prepares to crucify one of the two thieves.

In the foreground to the left Mary the mother of Jesus is comforted by other women. She cannot bring herself to watch her son while his cross is raised to its final position. The pain she feels is almost more than she can bear at the moment.

THE RAISING OF THE CROSS
Luca Giordano (Italian, 1632-1705);
Drawing: pen and ink; 46.8 x 70.1 cm. (18.3 x 27.3 in.);
Ailsa Mellon Bruce Fund

Crucifixion was a lingering and excruciatingly painful death. Sometimes the victims hung for days before succumbing, tortured by exhaustion and thirst. The body's blood drained to the lower extremities, putting an impossible strain on the heart while greatly distending the stomach. Because of the prior scourging and the extreme pain caused by the lack of support for the body's sagging weight, the victim soon developed fever and often became delirious.

Sometimes the victim was offered a drugged wine to help dull his suffering. Jesus was offered such a drug before he was raised to the cross; but after tasting it and discovering what it was, he spit it out, refusing any more.

Racked with intense pain and filled with terror, the victims usually shouted out curses on those who crucified them and on the mob that always gathered to watch an execution. So it was with one of the criminals crucified with Jesus. He turned his hatred on Jesus and belittled and mocked him. Jesus remained quiet, even serene. The words which finally broke from his lips when the soldiers nailed him to the crossbar were not the expected curse but a prayer for his tormenters: "Father, forgive them, for they know not what they do."

Then one of the robbers recognized something in Jesus which was different from all others. Perhaps he had heard Jesus preach somewhere in Galilee or Judea, or had seen him heal the afflicted. The true meaning of the sign above Jesus' head came to him, and he called out, "Lord, remember me when thou comest into thy kingdom." Jesus answered, "Today shalt thou be with me in paradise."

At the foot of the cross stood some of the women who had devotedly served Jesus during his years of public ministry. Mary, his mother, was among them, undoubtedly recalling those words of the aged Simeon when she presented her newborn son at the Temple: "Yea, a sword shall pierce through thy own soul also." Lovingly and tenderly Jesus commended Mary to the care of John, the beloved disciple, who stood there beside her.

As the soldiers drank their sour wine, the mob, led by the religious leaders, heckled Jesus. They derided him as a false Messiah, a fraud. The soldiers joined in, toasting "his majesty" and offering to share the toast with him. In dignity and quiet nobility, he refused.

THE SMALL CRUCIFIXION—This artist worked in southern Germany during the late fifteenth and early sixteenth centuries and painted powerful religious pictures. A contemporary of the younger Albrecht Dürer and an admirer of Martin Luther, Grünewald is best known today for the passionate vividness with which he portrays Jesus in his final agony on the cross.

In The Small Crucifixion, the artist shows Jesus grotesquely wrenched out of shape, his body deformed by dehumanizing agony. Jesus' flesh is lacerated and bloodied from his scourging. Here and there bits of bone or sharp spines from the Roman whips broken off in the scourging protrude, causing sharp pain with every movement. The grasping hands and twisted feet eloquently declare his anguish of spirit and physical pain.

Perhaps most moving of all is Jesus' hollow, drawn face as his head sags over his distended rib cage. His glazed eyes and open, ugly mouth seem to depict that moment of total spiritual abandonment when he cried out in despair, "My God, my God, why hast thou forsaken me?"

Jesus' mother stands beside the cross, shrouded in grief, while Mary Magdalene kneels by his feet. In three days' time she will again kneel at his feet, but then it will be in a garden outside his tomb, and she will be radiant with joy. The apostle John clasps his hands as though his heart will break; his face reflects his deep love for Jesus and the uncomprehending shock of watching his friend die horribly.

Grünewald contrasts darkness and light to emphasize both the horror of the event and the deep grief of John and the women.

THE SMALL CRUCIFIXION
Mathis Grünewald (German, c. 1465-1528);
Painting on wood; 61.6 x 46.0 cm. (24.0 x 17.9 in.);
Samuel H. Kress Collection 1961

CHRIST BETWEEN TWO THIEVES—In this magnificent etching Rembrandt shows those endless hours when Jesus and the two thieves hung, suspended between heaven and earth, slowly dying from pain and exhaustion. The soldiers stand guard, waiting for the moment of death to come. Their show of arms makes clear to all that Roman supremacy prevails, regardless of the ironic words on the sign which declare Jesus "King of the Jews."

The darkness which has settled over Jerusalem surrounds this place too, and it is only the eye of faith which can perceive light from above in the surrounding gloom. The thief on the right has called to Jesus for mercy, asking to be remembered in the kingdom of God, and Jesus has assured him that he will surely be that very day in paradise. A beam from heaven falls on his dying form, affirming the fulfillment of Jesus' promise.

The women and some disciples are grouped to the right of the cross, while the mob reacts with fear and wonder off to the left. In the center foreground two religious leaders walk away, pleased that their long night's work is over at last.

CRUCIFIXION—Moderno was a fifteenth century bronzemaster active in Padua, a major center for bronze work. This crucifixion is a small plaquette intended to inspire pious thoughts and to aid in prayer. It would have hung in the owner's private living quarters.

Moderno shows the two naked thieves tied to crosses, their bodies grotesquely distorted by pain. In contrast, Jesus is depicted almost in repose. This treatment of the crucifixion is inspired by the important works executed in Padua several decades earlier by the great Florentine sculptor Donatello.

In the lower left Mary, Jesus' mother, has swooned and is being held by some of his friends. Mary Magdalene grasps the cross with both arms, as she looks up with love and adoration. John the apostle stands to the left above the fallen Mary. The soldiers crowd around the crosses, mocking their victims and ensuring that the sentence is carried out to the full.

CRUCIFIXION
Moderno (Paduan, XV Century);
Bronze relief;
11.5 x 7.8 cm. (4.5 x 3.0 in.);
Samuel H. Kress Collection

CHRIST BETWEEN TWO THIEVES
Rembrandt van Rijn (Dutch, 1606-1669);
Etching; 38.5 x 45.0 cm. (15.0 x 17.6 in.);
Gift of R. Horace Gallatin

WARLICH DISER MENSCH IST GOTTES SVN GEWEST

Because death by crucifixion often took several days, and because the religious leaders wanted the bodies removed from the crosses before the beginning of the Passover festival, they sent a message to Pilate asking him to order the soldiers to break the victims' bones, thereby hastening their death. While this message and Pilate's answer were being conveyed back and forth, Jesus cried aloud, "Eli, Eli, lama sabachthani?" (in Aramaic, meaning "My God, my God, why hast thou forsaken me?"). Some thought he called out for Elijah to help him. Then he looked to heaven, and with the words, "Father, into thy hands I commend my spirit," he peacefully gave up his own life. When the centurion saw the impressive peace with which Jesus died, he admitted, "Truly this man was the Son of God."

By this time Pilate had agreed to the religious leaders' request. After the two robbers were brutally dispatched, the soldiers came to kill Jesus. They were surprised to find that he was already dead. To make sure, one of them thrust his short sword up through the stomach into the lung and heart. The blood and water which had collected in the stomach cavity over the hours gushed out. There was no need to break his bones. Jesus was dead.

THE CRUCIFIXION WITH LONGINUS
Lucas Cranach the Elder (German, 1472-1553);
Painting on wood; 50.8 x 34.9 cm. (19.8 x 13.6 in.);
Samuel H. Kress Collection

THE CRUCIFIXION WITH LONGINUS—Lucas Cranach, court painter to Frederick the Wise, Elector of Saxony, was so prolific an artist throughout his long life that his tombstone carries the words *Celerrimus pictor*, "Fastest Painter." In his later years the speed and volume of his work adversely affected the quality of his art. Not so, however, with this portrayal of the centurion Longinus gazing up at the crucified Jesus and affirming his faith. Cranach blended Gothic love for detail with Italian grace, and often added a touch of German humor. These elements are readily observed even in his treatment of so solemn a scene as the Crucifixion. Contrast the centurion's elegant hat here, a fashionable detail of court life, with the stark seriousness in Grünewald's treatment of the same subject (The Small Crucifixion), bearing in mind that these two artists were contemporaries.

Cranach possibly modeled the centurion after his patron, Elector Frederick. In parade armor, Longinus has reached his conclusion: "Truly this man was the Son of God." His horse rears, almost prances, commanding attention as the only moving force in the picture.

In the upper half of the scene the three men hang from their crosses. Jesus looks to heaven as he says, "Father, into thy hands I commend my spirit." The thief on the left looks to Jesus in faith, while the one on the right turns his head aside in bitter rejection. The three are theatrically highlighted against the darkness of those terrible hours.

THE PISTOIA CRUCIFIX—During the early seventeenth century Pietro Tacca, a Florentine, served as court sculptor to the grand dukes of Tuscany. He expressed the spirit of the early Baroque style with restraint and disciplined grace.

In The Pistoia Crucifix, Tacca has executed one of the most beautifully conceived versions of the crucifixion, a major theme for art of the Baroque era. His bronze figure of Jesus is attached to an aged, worm-eaten wooden cross, which has the INRI sign in a draped scroll placed above Jesus' head. The austere lines are heightened by gold leaf.

Tacca gives the dead Jesus movement and harmony of line, even in the stretched tendons and jutting ribcage, transforming him from a horribly scarred and battered victim of an agonizing death into an almost lyrical object of religious devotion.

There are many elements in the life of Jesus which have drawn people to reverence him. Some may be more attached to his ethical teachings; others to his example of love; others to the transforming effects of his power in their lives; and still others to the contemplation of his sufferings and his death on the cross. The crucifix has always been a cherished art form for those who are spiritually nourished by their meditation on the Passion of Jesus. For them, it is not so much the depiction of the dead Jesus which is central to the crucifix, for his resurrection is celebrated even as his death is remembered. Rather, the crucifix is a symbol of the mystery of his suffering for them, and for all people.

THE PISTOIA CRUCIFIX
Pietro Tacca (Florentine, 1577-1640);
Bronze;
Bronze height 86.9 cm. (33.9 in.); Cross height 166.9 cm. (65.1 in.);
Ailsa Mellon Bruce Fund 1974

Descent from the Cross

Jesus hung lifeless on the cross. Clustered in a tight circle below him, his mother and a small group of women who had accompanied him on his travels during his public ministry waited anxiously to see what would happen next. The women had provided much of Jesus' needs from their own resources, and now they stood with him and his mother to the end. The beloved disciple, John, was also there at the foot of the cross.

Two members of the Sanhedrin, Joseph of Arimathea and Nicodemus, secretly believed in Jesus and had not approved of the council's decision to have him put to death. Now they declared their faith openly. Joseph sought an interview with Pilate and begged for the body of Jesus. He wanted to bury him with dignity and in accordance with Jewish law. After Pilate ascertained that Jesus was indeed dead, expressing surprise that he had died so quickly, he permitted Joseph to take possession of the body.

Joseph and Nicodemus went with their servants to the place of crucifixion where, in the growing darkness of the evening, the servants unfastened Jesus' body from the cross and lowered it to the ground. Nicodemus had brought a hundred pounds of spices, a mixture of myrrh and aloes, to embalm the body. The small band of intimate mourners watched as Joseph and Nicodemus prepared Jesus' body for burial.

THE DESCENT FROM THE CROSS—Rembrandt expressed his deeply personal religious faith in his more than 250 paintings, etchings, and drawings based on biblical events. A member of the Dutch Reformed Church in his youth, he was greatly influenced in his mature years by the simplicity and spirituality of the Mennonites.

He painted The Descent from the Cross in 1651 while living in Amsterdam. During this period in his artistic development Rembrandt concentrated more on simplifying form than on elaborate detail. He focused directly on feelings, with less attention to movement. He increasingly used warmer, darker colors for subtle exploration of the emotional and spiritual dimensions of his subject.

The themes of divine and human love permeate Rembrandt's art. In this painting both are illuminated in the circle of light cast by the torch held in the hand of the man on the ladder. Rembrandt states his wonder at the mystery of Christ's loving gift of himself for the world by lighting Jesus' inert, grotesquely twisted body against the impending darkness of the night. Two men at the top of the cross tenderly lower the body into the arms of an old man, probably Nicodemus. Joseph of Arimathea, dressed in a luxuriant red turban and rich robes to emphasize his wealth and his importance in the Sanhedrin, directs this poignant event.

The disciples' hesitant hopes for some dramatic rescue from the cross had been bitterly disappointed; future resurrection was unimaginable; they were now engaged in the dark reality of taking down their Master's body and putting it forever in a tomb. Rembrandt shows Mary, Jesus' mother, staggering under the burden of this reality. As she collapses, she is lovingly held up by the other women who had come to this terrible moment with her. The hard, stark cross—with its cruel, rigid lines—contrasts dramatically with the love conveyed in human face and form.

THE DESCENT FROM THE CROSS
Rembrandt van Rijn (Dutch, 1606-1669); Painting on canvas; 143.0 x 111.0 cm. (55.8 x 43.3 in.);
Widener Collection 1942

THE DESCENT FROM THE CROSS
Vincenzo Danti (Florentine, 1530-1576);
Bronze sculpture; 44.5 x 47.1 cm. (17.4 x 18.4 in.);
Widener Collection 1942

THE DESCENT FROM THE CROSS—A gifted painter, sculptor, architect, and goldsmith Vincenzo Danti worked during the middle of the sixteenth century. Though a native of Umbria, he worked in Florence. His training as a goldsmith carried over into his work with bronze, which he treated with the attention to detail characteristic of objects crafted in malleable gold.

In The Descent from the Cross, Danti achieves remarkable depth of focus. In the center Joseph and some of the soldiers lower the body of Jesus. Some hold his limbs; others use cords to keep him from falling to the ground. In the mannered style of many sixteenth century artists Danti often elongated his figures; he did so here with the body of Jesus as well as with some of the women.

On the right Mary swoons. As her knees buckle, she is supported by the other women, who rush to her aid. In the background the two thieves still hang on their crosses.

THE DEPOSITION—This etching of the Thirteenth Station of the Cross shows the deposition, the taking down of the lifeless Jesus from the cross. Tiepolo fills the scene with openly expressed emotion and with powerful drama.

John stands weeping unabashedly. Mary is inconsolable in her grief as she swoons beside her son's body, which is beginning to take on the stiffness and pallor of death. Two men lean over the body as they begin to wrap it in a shroud. Mary Magdalene stares through tear-swollen eyes from behind Jesus' mother. In the center rear Joseph of Arimathea watches the scene. Jesus' enemies and executors have all departed, and at this moment he is surrounded only by those who love him.

THE DEPOSITION
Giandomenico Tiepolo (Venetian, 1727-1804); Etching; 21.6 x 17.2 cm. (8.4 x 6.7 in.);
Rosenwald Collection

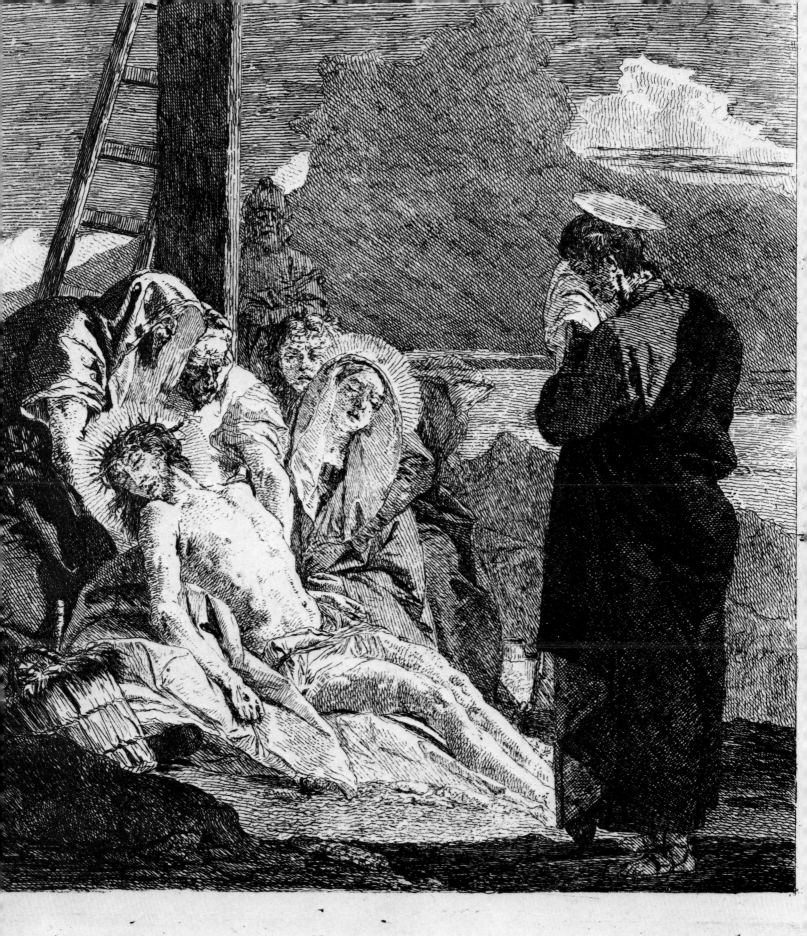

STAZIONE XIII.

MORTO GESÙ, VIEN DEPOSTO DALLA CROCE IN SENO ALLA SUA SS.ᴬ MADRE.

Spira del Padre in sen L'Alma adorata

Gesù: resta a Maria La Spoglia amata.

Pieta

Although not specifically mentioned in Scripture, Mary's lamenting over the body of Jesus after he was taken down from the cross is an entirely plausible event which has a long tradition in the history of art as well as in popular religious devotion.

Some art portrays Mary cradling Jesus in her lap at that last moment of human contact before his body is taken away to the tomb. Michelangelo's *Pieta* is the best-known, and perhaps the most moving, example of this scene. It would surely have been instinctive for Mary to want to hold the battered body of her son. Her falling tears would wash away some of the crusted blood from his wounds.

One can only ponder with caution what went through her mind. Neither she, nor any around her, knew that Jesus' death was not final; his resurrection was three days away. For all they knew he was finally and irrevocably dead. Both his life and his mission were at an end. It seemed true enough that he could heal others, even raise some from the dead, but could not save himself from the grave.

Did Mary think back on her son's remarkable life? Did she remember the angel's visit, telling her that she would bear the Messiah? And then wonder how it was that she now held a lifeless body in her arms? Did she recall the moment when he was twelve and she discovered him in the Temple, astounding the religious leaders with his knowledge and insight? And then shake her head in confusion when these same leaders condemned him to his death? Did she think back to his miraculous raising from the dead of the widow's son at Nain, of the young girl in Capernaum, and of Lazarus in Bethany only a week earlier? Did she wonder how it could be all over now?

THE LAMENTATION OF THE VIRGIN—Marcantonio Raimondi was an early sixteenth century Italian master engraver whose clear line and form were easy for apprentices to duplicate. Several engravers in a studio could work together on a single plate, increasing their output under the artistic direction of a single master. Raimondi and his followers were especially successful in giving the feeling of sculptural form or bulk to figures. Their broad, dark cross-hatchings gave an open effect, somewhat like a woodcut, to engravings.

The Lamentation of the Virgin depicts a grieving Mary standing over the body of her son. She looks heavenward, or perhaps inward, with no answer to her question, "Why has this happened?" She was not the first mother to mourn a son violently killed, nor has she been the last. But because of the character of her son and of his death, Mary's lamentation can poignantly represent all mothers who ask that unanswerable question.

The body of Jesus lies serenely on a low stone wall. His time of suffering is past; it is as though he waits in peace for resurrection from the dead. The dark opening in the cliff suggests the tomb into which his body will soon be placed.

In the distance the soldiers return to the city, their task finished. When evening falls, they will be needed to keep public order after this tumultuous day, with the throngs of worshipers in Jerusalem for the Passover. Mary too will return, taking back to Jerusalem memories of her son and her somber awareness of the reality of his death.

THE LAMENTATION OF THE VIRGIN
Marcantonio Raimondi (Italian, c. 1480-1530); Engraving; 33.1 x 22.3 cm. (12.9 x 8.7 in.);
Rosenwald Collection

The Burial of Jesus

Joseph of Arimathea owned a new burial chamber close to Golgotha. He had intended it as his own final resting place, but now found a more urgent use for it. He and Nicodemus, both members of the Sanhedrin who had not consented to the death of Jesus, directed their servants as they prepared Jesus' body for burial in Joseph's unused tomb. They had to work quickly in order to have the tomb sealed prior to sunset, the start of the Passover Sabbath.

Following age-old Jewish tradition, they probably first bathed Jesus' body with water. Then they carefully wrapped it with strips of clean white cloth, placing the myrrh and aloes that Nicodemus had brought in between the long strips of cloth as they bound them around the body. Aloes was a precious spice used to perfume garments; now it would counteract the smell of decomposition. Myrrh was a rare ingredient in holy anointing oil and was often used in rare cosmetics; now it added its sweet fragrance to Jesus' body.

They carried the body of Jesus to the nearby tomb. This was a shallow chamber cut from the side of a steep hill composed of solid rock. Large enough to hold only a single body on a ledge hewn from the rock, the tomb was accessible only through an opening so low that a man had to stoop to enter.

The women, including Mary the mother of Jesus and Mary Magdalene, had followed every move since Jesus' body was taken down from the cross. They watched with broken hearts as the men carried the wrapped body the short distance to Joseph's tomb. They waited outside the low doorway opening as the men placed the body inside on the ledge. Then they saw the men roll a large circular stone over the opening, sealing the tomb. The stone settled into position with a finality that said louder than any words, "It is over."

The religious leaders remembered that Jesus had said he would rise from the dead. Although they thought this nonsense, they wanted to protect themselves against possible fraud. They prevailed on Pontius Pilate to provide a guard to ensure the security of the tomb. As the soldiers took their place, doubtless grumbling at what seemed a senseless assignment, the women slipped away into the growing darkness of the evening. It was indeed over.

THE ENTOMBMENT
Albrecht Dürer (German, 1471-1528);
Drawing: pen and ink;
29.2 x 21.0 cm. (11.4 x 8.2 in.);
Syma Busiel Fund

THE ENTOMBMENT—Dürer drew The Entombment in 1504 (note the date on the lid of the stone coffin in the center of the drawing), a decade after he had first visited Italy. He shows the knowledge of anatomy he gained there, as well as a fluidity of line and the ability to give perspective.

One of the servants of Joseph of Arimathea is lifting the body of Jesus to place it in the sarcophagus. The body is inert, heavy, and the servant strains to get leverage. Mary Magdalene kneels at Jesus' feet, bestowing her farewell kiss on those feet she once washed with her tears and dried with her hair. Mary, Jesus' mother, kneels with her hands lifted in prayer; her eyes stare at this last, incredible event. The apostle John rests his hand on her shoulder, bound to her in the grief they share and in the new responsibility for each other which Jesus gave to them during those last moments on the cross. Just as Mary is lost in the privacy of her own thoughts, so too John stares unseeingly at the waiting tomb.

Nicodemus stands behind the women, holding the jar of spices he has brought to anoint the body. Joseph of Arimathea is beside him, talking to a servant about the next step in readying the body for burial. Dürer suggests the proximity of the tomb to the Place of the Skull by showing the three crosses on a nearby hill; only the body of Jesus has been removed.

THE ENTOMBMENT—Andrea Riccio was a Paduan bronzemaster of the early sixteenth century. At the end of a successful career, he fell under suspicion of sympathizing with the Reformation. His ecclesiastical commissions stopped, and when he died, he was refused the last sacraments of his church.

Riccio shows the body of Jesus being lowered into a sarcophagus by Nicodemus and Joseph of Arimathea, assisted by the apostle John. We see the wound caused by the sword thrust in the lower abdomen and the nail prints in the feet. Jesus alone seems at peace; all the others express by their faces and their bodies the deep anguish they feel. Mary Magdalene kneels at Jesus' feet, caressing them in a final act of adoration. Mary, the mother of Jesus, lifts her arms in mourning, as one of the other women stands comfortingly behind her. There is a terrible finality to this moment, expressed best by the hopelessness of Mary's upraised arms. Jesus is dead.

THE ENTOMBMENT
Andrea Riccio (Paduan, 1470-1532); Bronze relief; 14.5 x 20.8 cm. (5.7 x 8.1 in.);
Samuel H. Kress Collection

CHRIST CARRIED TO THE TOMB
Rembrandt van Rijn (Dutch, 1606-1669);
Etching;
13.0 x 10.7 cm. (5.1 x 4.2 in.);
Rosenwald Collection

CHRIST CARRIED TO THE TOMB—In spare, deft strokes Rembrandt captures the inexpressibly sad moment when Jesus' body is borne to the entrance of the tomb. The bearers carry out their silent duty with downcast heads. Anyone who has borne the body of a friend to its grave knows the lonely melancholy of this task. One bearer, perhaps Joseph of Arimathea who has given his own tomb, looks down tenderly on the face of Jesus. That face is a lifeless mask; the vibrant, loving Jesus they knew, filled so often with compassion or indignation, is gone. Only the shell remains. Rembrandt suggests this lifeless shell by even so minute a detail as the angle of Jesus' foot as it dangles from the bier.

The mother of Jesus walks directly behind his body. Her eyes are hollow with exhaustion, yet the set of her head suggests she will see this terrible event through to the end. Time enough later for tears and the working out of her grief. Now she will bury her son. The other women crowd in, weeping with a sense of irreparable loss.

The goal of this sad procession is at the left, a gaping hole carved out of the rocky hillside. Inside a narrow ledge of stone had been hewn to receive Joseph of Arimathea. Now, instead of the body of an honored member of the Sanhedrin, the ledge will hold the body of a despised, crucified criminal who claimed to be the Messiah.

RESURRECTION

AND
ASCENSION

THE THREE MARYS AT THE TOMB
Unknown (German, 1460-1480);
Metalcut; 6.2 x 4.6 cm. (2.4 x 1.8 in.);
Rosenwald Collection

The Empty Tomb

During the long Sabbath Jesus' followers began to regroup themselves after the shock of his arrest, trial, and crucifixion. The Sabbath proved to be a rest for their fevered spirits, and they began to accept the reality of his death. They made the upper room where the Last Supper had been held their center.

Several of the women prepared further to anoint Jesus' body with spices early in the morning after the Sabbath. They wondered how they could shift the heavy stone away from the tomb's opening. To their great surprise, they found it already rolled back. They cautiously entered, uncertain of what they might find. A young man, radiantly clothed in a long white garment, sat inside. He spoke reassuringly to the now terrified women: "Ye seek Jesus of Nazareth, which was crucified: he is risen; he is not here: behold the place where they laid him." The winding sheets in which Joseph of Arimathea had wrapped Jesus' body lay on the ledge. The cloth which had covered his head was neatly folded at the end.

Ecstatic with joy at the angel's message and convinced by the sight of the empty grave clothes, the women ran off to tell the disciples. Only Mary Magdalene remained behind. While she stood in the garden outside the tomb, she met a man whom she presumed to be the gardener. With heaviness of heart she explained that someone had taken the body of Jesus away, and she asked whether he knew anything about what had happened. He looked deeply into her eyes and said simply, "Mary." She knew at once it was Jesus who spoke to her. On his instructions she too went to tell the disciples.

Peter and John hurried to the tomb to see for themselves. When they arrived at the entrance, John, who got there first, stooped over and saw it was as the women had reported. Peter came rushing up and, characteristically, went into the tomb to see for himself. They then returned to Jerusalem to inform the others.

The guards reported their experience to the Sanhedrin. We do not know exactly what they saw when the stone was rolled away and Jesus came out from the tomb. The religious leaders, however, gave them money to testify that they had slept while on duty and that the disciples had come at night to steal the body. The leaders also promised the guards that they would handle matters with Pilate if he heard any report that his troops had been asleep when they should have been on watch.

CHRIST APPEARING
TO MARY MAGDALENE
Martin Schongauer
(German, c. 1450-1491);
Engraving;
15.8 x 15.6 cm.
(6.2 x 6.1 in.);
Rosenwald Collection

CHRIST APPEARING TO MARY MAGDALENE—The late fifteenth century master engraver Martin Schongauer shows Jesus with Mary Magdalene at the moment he has called her by name. Instantly she recognized this stranger and fell on her knees, exclaiming, "Master." She was about to clasp his feet in adoration, but he cautioned her not to touch him. A new relationship is to replace their previous friendship. The risen Jesus is soon to ascend to the Father, fully and openly to participate in the divine nature. Jesus gently prepares Mary to accept this next step.

Schongauer shows the garden enclosed by a wicket of saplings, a kind of construction common in a land of forests like Germany. The lone tree in this garden is dead, a reference to Christ's own experience of death which is now forever at an end. Mary's jar of spices stands unused on the ground beside her. She reaches out to touch her newfound Master, but he stays her hand. The marks of his crucifixion appear on his feet and on his breast. He stands solidly on the ground, still flesh and bone, and yet his face is godlike. He carries on his staff the cross, symbol of his death; from it flies the banner of his church, also marked by a cross. With the Resurrection the cross has become a sign of ultimate victory, not of death.

THE RESURRECTION — Pieter Brueghel I ("The Elder") was a sixteenth century painter and designer of engravings. His sons, Pieter and Jan, continued to work in his tradition, but he stands clearly as one of the greatest Flemish artists of all time. Brueghel often painted human figures in a grotesque manner in order to satirize human folly. He adapted this use of the fantastic from his famous contemporary, Hieronymus Bosch. He also tended to show figures from the back, or at least with their faces partly covered. He was an early believer in "body language," convinced that more could be learned from the cast of the entire body than from the face alone. His figures are generally types rather than individuals.

The Resurrection brings several elements of the biblical narrative together. The sun rises beyond the city of Jerusalem. The women have come from the city bearing their spices. Their mission is a mournful one, and their bodies convey heaviness of spirit. The angel sits on the stone, waiting to tell them the good news of Jesus' resurrection. Behind the angel Jesus himself rises from the tomb, a second center of light. He is triumphant over death and sin, bearing his standard of victory. The soldiers, who thought they had everything under control, are stupefied. Some sleep; some are stunned; some search for evidence of the missing body. Armed with weapons of sixteenth century Europe, they are powerless before the power of the risen Jesus.

THE RESURRECTION
Pieter Brueghel the Elder (Flemish, 1528-1569);
Engraving;
45.8 x 32.1 cm. (17.9 x 12.5 in.);
Rosenwald Collection

THE RESURRECTION
Benvenuto di Giovanni (Sienese, 1436-c. 1518); Painting on wood; 43.2 x 48.9 cm. (16.8 x 19.1 in.);
Samuel H. Kress Collection 1939

THE RESURRECTION—This imaginative picturing of the moment of resurrection by the fifteenth century Sienese artist Benvenuto di Giovanni shows the Roman guard in total disarray.

Jesus has just burst forth from the sealed tomb. Although the nail prints appear in his hand, he is shown with regal bearing and youthful vigor. Gone entirely are the bruises on his body and his agony of spirit. This is the risen, triumphant Jesus, who has conquered death. He holds the standard of his victory, as he raises his right hand in benediction.

The stone has crashed to the ground. The guards are struck dumb with terror, their hands clutching air as they are convulsed with panic, their eyes bulging at the unexpected, unimaginable sight. They are the first to see the risen Lord, and the vision unnerves them. These are tough legionnaires who have seen hundreds die in battle and who have probably crucified many prisoners. Death is their trade, and though they know the fear of death, they now experience the fear of God who can overcome mortality.

CHRIST ON THE ROAD TO EMMAUS
Unknown (American, c. 1720-1740); Painting on canvas; 64.7 x 78.2 cm. (25.2 x 30.5 in.);
Gift of Edgar William and Bernice Chrysler Garbisch

The Road to Emmaus

Later that day two disciples were walking to the small village of Emmaus, about seven miles away from Jerusalem. They had heard the women's report of the empty tomb, corroborated by Peter and John. As they walked, they were discussing what had happened in Jerusalem since Jesus first arrived there a week before.

A stranger joined them and asked what they were talking about that made them so sad. This "stranger" was Jesus, but, distracted by their grief and confusion, the two disciples failed to recognize him. Instead, they looked at him with some astonishment, and commented that he must be the only person in the

CHRIST ON THE ROAD TO EMMAUS—In this charming painting by an unknown itinerant artist of eighteenth century America, Jesus is shown walking along a country road with two disciples. The setting could well be upstate New York, perhaps the Mohawk Valley with the placid Mohawk River flowing in the background. Beyond the river is a solid homestead, much like those established by the sturdy Dutch who were the first Europeans to settle this region.

The artist shows the two disciples listening intently while Christ expounds the meaning of the Hebrew Scriptures as they illumine his own life and mission. Perhaps the disciple with the hat is Cleopas, the disciple named in the Bible.

Religious subjects are rare in early American art. The American colonists generally preferred portraits to narrative painting of any kind, and itinerant artists, sometimes referred to as "face limners," often traveled with half-finished canvases to which they had only to add the subject's features. The artist here shows considerable skill in situating his figures in the landscape and articulating the drama of their gestures, movements, and facial expressions. He seems familiar with the great masters of Italy and France, although perhaps only at second hand.

whole region who was not aware of what had happened to Jesus of Nazareth. Then they told him of Jesus' arrest, trial, execution, and burial, and how the women had found the tomb empty.

With gentle, mock-serious chiding, Jesus said: "O fools, and slow of heart to believe all that the prophets have spoken: Ought not Christ to have suffered these things, and to enter into his glory?" Then he explained to them how the whole body of Hebrew Scriptures—from Moses through all the prophets—spoke of him in one form or another.

They came to Emmaus as he was finishing, and he seemed ready to travel farther. The disciples pressed him to stay with them, since it was now getting dark, and share their evening meal. They wanted to hear more from this remarkable teacher, whom they still failed to recognize.

As they sat together at table, Jesus took bread, broke it, and blessed it. At this moment the two disciples realized who he was. Then suddenly he was no longer there. They returned immediately to Jerusalem, found the eleven apostles in the upper room, and told how Jesus became known to them in the breaking of the bread.

CHRIST AT EMMAUS
Rembrandt van Rijn (Dutch, 1606-1669);
Etching and drypoint;
21.2 x 16.0 cm. (8.3 x 6.2 in.);
Gift of W.G. Russell Allen

CHRIST AT EMMAUS—Rembrandt has set the figures in his etching on a platform before a regal drapery, like a eucharistic celebration at a richly decorated altar. Only a hint of vine at the right and the post of a rustic staircase suggest that this is taking place in a country inn.

Jesus has just broken the bread and blessed it; he now gives each a portion. In this act the two disciples recognize who he is. The one on the right, who still sits, lifts his hands in astonishment, delighted but overawed. The disciple on the left rises wonderingly to his feet, probably unconscious of his movement. He folds his hands in front of his face as he gazes at Jesus in joy and worship. The servant, who has just brought the food, does not know why these two are reacting as they do, and so he turns to head back to the kitchen, trying to figure out what makes the man who broke the bread so special. The dog unconcernedly keeps an open eye out for scraps that might come his way.

Jesus is the center of the composition. By using only a few lines for his face and torso and by surrounding him with darker lines and cross-hatching, Rembrandt gives him a blinding radiance. Yet this Jesus is not regally aloof, nor is he like an unearthly spirit; he is solid, a commanding presence. He holds out a piece of bread in each hand. His face is thoughtful, confident, and very gentle. These two disciples will never forget the depth of his patient love for them.

Jesus Appears to the Disciples

After his resurrection from the dead Jesus appeared to his disciples a number of times over a period of forty days. Some of these appearances occurred immediately in Judea; some later in Galilee.

He appeared to the two on the road to Emmaus the day of his resurrection. As these two reported to the apostles in the upper room, Jesus suddenly appeared. They were terrified, wondering whether he was a ghost. His words calmed them: "Peace be unto you." He showed them his hands and feet, and the wound in his side, to assure them that it was really he. Then he asked for food in order to demonstrate beyond question that he was no ghost. And he taught them all about himself from the Scriptures, as he had taught the two on that walk to Emmaus.

Thomas was not present at this appearance. This Thomas had a twin brother (we do not know who this brother was) so he is often called Didymus, "The Twin." When he heard from the other apostles about Jesus' appearance, he expressed his doubt, affirming that he would never believe this story unless he put his fingers in the nail prints and his hand in the wound in Jesus' side.

A week later all the apostles were in the same closed upper room, Thomas among them, when Jesus once again appeared. He called on Thomas to reach out and put his finger in the nail prints and thrust his hand into the wound in his side. Overwhelmed with emotion, awed in the presence of the risen Jesus, Thomas fell on his knees and confessed, "My Lord and my God!" Jesus then pronounced a blessing—some have it called the last and best beatitude—on all those who, unlike Thomas, would come to faith without seeing. "Thomas, because thou hast seen me, thou hast believed: blessed are they that have not seen, and yet have believed."

THE APPARITION OF CHRIST AMONG THE APOSTLES
Bramantino (Milanese, c. 1465-1530); Painting on wood; 23.8 x 19.5 cm. (9.3 x 7.6 in.);
Samuel H. Kress Collection 1961

THE APPARITION OF CHRIST AMONG THE APOSTLES—Bartolommeo Suardi, called Bramantino, was one of the chief painters of early sixteenth century Milan. After Leonardo da Vinci left Milan in 1494, Bramantino became for a generation the leading painter of the city. He was also an architect; this interest shows itself in his art.

In The Apparition of Christ Among the Apostles he shows Jesus' appearance in the upper room in Jerusalem. Six of the apostles can be seen; perhaps the two to the right are Peter and John. Are they discussing their discovery of the empty tomb earlier that morning? Jesus reaches forward to them, his arm on John's back and his hand on Peter's arm as he gives them physical, tangible assurance that he is not a vision.

John appears enraptured at the return of his Lord; he retained that love until he died a very old man, tradition-ally the bishop of Ephesus. Jesus looks steadily and supportively into Peter's eyes, assuring him that his love and trust have not been dashed by Peter's denial. Peter would become a primary leader of the early Christian church, steadfast and energetic to the end, when he was crucified in the city of Rome.

This moment of encounter between Jesus and two chief disciples sets the course of future history, for they will boldly testify from this time on that they have seen the risen Lord. It is this message that will establish the Christian church.

Two more disciples hurry forward to hear what is being said. The faint outlines of other disciples can be seen in the room. Soon Jesus will join them all, and breathe on them as he says, "Receive ye the Holy Ghost." Thus he empowers them to undertake the Great Commission of telling the story of Jesus in all the world.

CHRIST APPEARING TO HIS DISCIPLES
Valerio Belli (Italian, c. 1468-1546);
Bronze relief; 10.7 x 6.6 cm. (4.2 x 2.6 in.);
Samuel H. Kress Collection

CHRIST APPEARING TO HIS DISCIPLES—This mid-sixteenth century bronze plaque by the Italian gem carver Valerio Belli shows Christ appearing in the upper room to the ten apostles soon after the Resurrection. Thomas the Twin is absent on this occasion.

Christ is depicted as a king triumphant over death, holding his staff with its cross and banner, symbols of his victory over the grave. The beams that radiate from him take the form of the cross on which he died. The disciples are astonished at his sudden presence in their midst. He quiets their apprehension by saying, "Peace be unto you." Belli captures those words above the arch: Pax Vobis.

The disciples crowd around Jesus, somewhat fearful yet eager to learn all they can of the meaning of his resurrection and its impact on their own future.

THE INCREDULITY OF ST. THOMAS—
When Dürer died in 1528 at the age of fifty-seven, he left enough woodcuts, engravings, and drawings to support his widow in comfort for many years. He was a prolific worker who captured in his art the realities of his generation: the fears and joys of people, their weaknesses and strengths, beauty and ugliness.

The Incredulity of St. Thomas shows the company of apostles in the upper room. This is one week after Jesus' first appearance, when Thomas was absent. Thomas had expressed his doubt about the Resurrection, affirming that he would believe it only if he could touch with his own fingers Jesus' wounds.

Now Jesus appears again to them, even though the door to the room is closed and locked. He goes immediately to Thomas, takes his wrist, and thrusts Thomas' fingers into the wound in his side. The nail prints in his hands and feet are clearly visible. Thomas, the greatest doubter among the twelve, has come to the strongest and clearest confession of faith as with joy he declares, "My Lord and my God!"

THE INCREDULITY OF ST. THOMAS
Albrecht Dürer (German, 1471-1528);
Woodcut; 12.8 x 8.5 cm. (5.0 x 3.3 in.);
Rosenwald Collection

Soon after Jesus appeared to the eleven in the upper room in Jerusalem, several of the disciples who were Galileans went north to their own homes along the shores of Lake Galilee. In this quiet, familiar setting, a locale where Jesus had taught and healed for so many months, perhaps they could hope to find their bearings in this strange post-resurrection world. One evening Peter announced that he was going fishing; Thomas, Nathanael, James, John, and two others decided to join him. They launched their small boat, hoisted sail, and set off to one of their favorite fishing spots in the lake. How refreshing it was to ply their old trade, to be doing something so second-nature after the three years with Jesus so full of surprise and, at the end, high emotional stress.

All night long they worked, casting their nets where they knew the fish ran, yet catching not a one. In the early morning light, when they were about one hundred yards off the shore, they made out the shape of a man standing near the edge of the water cooking his breakfast over a small fire. He called out to them and asked if they had caught anything. Not a thing, they answered. He told them to try the starboard side once more; they did, and were unable to haul in their net, so great was the catch. Peter knew at once it was Jesus. "It is the Lord," he shouted, jumped into the water and swam to land. The others landed nearby and dragged the net ashore. They counted one hundred and fifty-three fish, more than enough to damage a net, though theirs was not torn.

Jesus invited them to have breakfast with him. He had fish and bread enough for all. After they had eaten, he asked Peter, calling him by his old name of Simon, "Lovest thou me?" Peter said he did. "Feed my lambs," responded Jesus. Three times this sequence was repeated, putting Peter's threefold denial of Jesus forever into the past. Jesus hinted that Peter's faithfulness in feeding the sheep, or caring for the flock of God, would eventually lead to crucifixion. Tradition tells us that, years later, Peter was indeed crucified in Rome.

This peaceful meeting by Lake Galilee at dawn was a major step in transforming timid disciples into bold apostles, in changing Galilean fishermen into fishers of men. These men would soon undertake the work for which Jesus had trained them so thoroughly during the past three years.

Jesus in Galilee

CHRIST AT THE SEA OF GALILEE
Tintoretto (Venetian, 1518-1594);
Painting on canvas; 117.0 x 168.5 cm. (45.6 x 65.7 in.);
Samuel H. Kress Collection 1952

CHRIST AT THE SEA OF GALILEE—Jacopo Robusti, better known as Tintoretto, was born in 1518, the son of a Venetian dyer. He wanted only to be a painter, and was apprenticed briefly to Titian at the age of twelve. He was soon dismissed either for reasons of carelessness or jealousy, and was forced to teach himself. His ideal was to blend the draftsmanship of Michelangelo and the color of Titian with his own compelling fascination for the people he saw daily in Venice, a major center of world commerce and banking at the time. The name Tintoretto means "little dyer (*tintor*)," an affectionate play on both his parentage and his magnificent, lavish use of color in his art.

Tintoretto often worked on ceiling frescoes. He fashioned wax models of his figures and drew them from every possible angle. He even hung them from the ceiling so he could study them from that angle. This often resulted in elongated perspectives which, together with his dramatic use of light and dark, yielded an astonishingly dramatic picture. Given a story to narrate, Tintoretto typically gave it a vivid natural backdrop and imbued it with restless vitality through his dazzling painting techniques. All of these characteristics can be seen in Christ at the Sea of Galilee. The risen Jesus, a figure of commanding power and authority, stands at the shoreline of the storm-tossed lake. One can feel the wind blowing and smell the roiled water. In the breaking morning light, clouds scud past. Peter has recognized Jesus and is about to leap into the water to go to him. The other six disciples busy themselves with controlling the boat and managing their net.

151

The Ascension

On the fortieth day after his resurrection Jesus met with a group of his disciples on the Mount of Olives just above the village of Bethany. We do not know who were there exactly, but we can presume those present included the eleven, Mary his mother, Mary and Martha and Lazarus of Bethany, and John Mark and his family from Jerusalem. There may have been well over a hundred people. Jesus gathered them about and told them they should wait in Jerusalem until they were given power from on high through the baptism of the Holy Spirit.

They still wanted to know if he would soon establish his kingdom on earth. Jesus told them that the time for establishing the kingdom in its final form was a matter only God the Father could determine. They were not to waste time and energy speculating on a matter which was beyond their control. However, he did give them a clear-cut task: "Ye shall receive power, after that the Holy Ghost is come upon you; and ye shall be witnesses unto me both in Jerusalem, and in all Judea, and in Samaria, and unto the uttermost part of the earth."

After giving this great commission, Jesus rose for a distance off the ground. His body seemed to become translucent, and then transparent, and he vanished into what appeared to be a cloud or mist. He had vanished from their presence for the last time. As his disciples gazed up into the sky, searching for any trace of their beloved Lord, two angels in gleaming white garments stood by them. The angels, messengers from the Most High, spoke to those wondering disciples in words which have sustained faith ever since: "Why stand ye gazing up into heaven? This same Jesus, which is taken up from you into heaven, shall so come in like manner as ye have seen him go into heaven."

As the disciples returned to Jerusalem, they remembered how Jesus looked lovingly down on them as he ascended. Their mood was not one of sorrow at having lost a friend, but of joy at having new hope to face all their tomorrows.

THE ASCENSION—Johann Koerbecke was a minor fifteenth century German artist who worked mostly in Münster. He was strongly influenced by the Flemish school, but retained many traditional German Gothic traits. The faces on his figures are vividly North German.

Koerbecke fills his painting with the symbolism so beloved by Gothic artists. The disciples watch with awe as Jesus ascends to heaven. A disciple named Matthias has been added to the eleven, chosen by lot to replace Judas Iscariot. Matthias, like the others, had been with Jesus from the beginning of his public ministry and had been a witness of the risen Jesus. The artist shows tongues of fire rising from the heads of the apostles, suggesting the power of the Holy Spirit which would fall on them at Pentecost.

Mary kneels in a posture of adoration of her ascended son. She is a model of faith for all who would also worship Jesus. The apostle John places his arm protectively around her, true to the charge given him to care for her to the end of her life. Peter kneels opposite Mary, his arms reaching out in an active expression of worship. The footprints in the stone are a traditional device to suggest that the Jesus who is seen in the heavens has risen there from the earth.

Jesus carries the staff with cross and banner of his victory over death. He sits in regal pose as the King of Heaven, who now bestows his blessing on his followers below. Already he seems remote, even aloof, in this new relationship. Note the nail print in his hand and the wound in his side.

Just as the apostles and Mary on earth witnessed his ascension, so too did the Hebrew kings and prophets whom the artist places in heaven. Among those Old Testament saints one can readily identify King David, with crown and harp, and Moses, with the Tables of the Law.

THE ASCENSION
Johann Koerbecke (German, active 1453-1491);
Painting on wood; 92.5 x 64.8 cm. (36.1 x 25.3 in.);
Samuel H. Kress Collection 1959

INDEX

In this index of **The Illustrated Life of Jesus from The National Gallery of Art Collection**, the narratives about events in the life of Jesus appear in boldface; the names of paintings and other pieces of art appear in italics; and the names of artists appear in roman type. Where more than one piece of art has the same name, the name of the artist appears in parentheses.

SCRIPTURE INDEX

BIRTH AND CHILDHOOD

The Annunciation: *Luke 1:26-38*
Mary Visits Elizabeth: *Luke 1:39-56*
The Birth of John: *Luke 1:57-80*
Mary and Joseph Are Married: *Matthew 1:18-24*
The Birth of Jesus: *Matthew 1:25; Luke 2:1-7*
The Shepherds' Visit: *Luke 2:8-20*
The Presentation: *Luke 2:21-38*
The Visit of the Magi: *Matthew 2:1-12*
The Flight into Egypt: *Matthew 2:13-15*
Childhood
The Massacre of the Innocents: *Matthew 2:16-23*
Jesus Visits Jerusalem, Age 12: *Luke 2:41-52*

THE MINISTRY

The Ministry of John the Baptist: *Matthew 3:1-12; Mark 1:1-8; Luke 3:1-18; John 1:19-28*
The Baptism of Jesus: *Matthew 3:13-17; Mark 1:9-11; Luke 3:21-22; John 1:29-34*
The Temptation of Jesus: *Matthew 4:1-11; Mark 1:12-13; Luke 4:1-13*
The First Disciples: *Matthew 4:18-22; Mark 1:16-20; Luke 5:1-11; John 1:35-42*
The Marriage at Cana: *John 2:1-11*
The Cleansing of the Temple: *Matthew 21:12-13; Mark 11:15-17; Luke 19:45-46; John 2:13-21*
Nicodemus Visits Jesus: *John 3:1-21*
The Samaritan Woman: *John 4:1-42*
Teaching and Healing: *Matthew 4:23-25, Mark 1:21-2:12; Luke 5:17-26, 6:17-19, John 5:17-26; and throughout the Gospels*
The Death of John the Baptist: *Matthew 14:1-12; Mark 6:14-29; Luke 9:7-9*
Jesus Walks on Water: *Matthew 14:22-33; Mark 6:45-52; John 6:15-21*
The Transfiguration: *Matthew 17:1-13; Mark 9:2-13; Luke 9:28-36*
The Woman Taken in Adultery: *John 8:1-11*
The Raising of Lazarus: *John 11:1-57*
Mary Magdalene: *Matthew 26:6-13; Mark 14:3-9; John 12: 1-8*

SCRIPTURE INDEX

THE LAST WEEK

Triumphal Entry into Jerusalem: *Matthew 21:1-11; Mark 11:1-11; Luke 19:28-40; John 12:1-19*

Washing of the Feet: *John 13:1-20*

The Last Supper: *Matthew 26:17-30; Mark 14:12-26; Luke 22:3-30; John 13:21-30*

Agony in the Garden: *Matthew 26:36-46; Mark 14:32-42; Luke 22:39-46*

Betrayal and Arrest: *Matthew 26:17-56; Mark 14:43-50; Luke 22:47-53; John 18:1-12*

Peter's Denial: *Matthew 26:57-58, 69-75; Mark 14:53-54, 66-72; Luke 22:54-62; John 18:12-18, 25-27*

Before Annas: *John 11:45-53; see also Matthew 26:57-66; Mark 14:53-64; John 18:12-13, cf. 18:33, 19:12*

Before Herod Antipas: *Luke 23:6-12*

The Scourging of Jesus: *Matthew 27:20-26; Mark 15:6-15; Luke 23:20-23; John 18:28-30, 19:1*

Crowning with Thorns: *Matthew 27:27-31; Mark 15:16-20; John 18:36, 19:2-3*

Ecce Homo: *John 19:4-9*

Condemnation to Death: *Matthew 27:15-26; Mark 15:6-15; Luke 23:13-25; John 19:8-16*

The Way of the Cross: *Matthew 27:32-33; Mark 15:21-22; Luke 23:26-31; John 19:16-17*

The Crucifixion: *Matthew 27:33-56; Mark 15:22-40; Luke 23:32-49; John 19:18-37*

Descent from the Cross: *Matthew 27:55-61; Mark 15:40-47; Luke 23:48-56; John 19:25, 38-42*

The Burial of Jesus: *Matthew 27:59-61; Mark 15:46-47; Luke 23:53-56; John 19:40-42*

RESURRECTION AND ASCENSION

The Empty Tomb: *Matthew 28:1-10; Mark 16:1-11; Luke 24:1-12; John 20: 1-8*

The Road to Emmaus: *Mark 16:12-13; Luke 24:13-35*

Jesus Appears to the Disciples: *Matthew 28:16-20; Mark 16:14-18; Luke 24:36-49; John 20:19-29*

Jesus in Galilee: *John 21:1-19*

The Ascension: *Acts 1:1-11*